Rev. E. W. Sprague

Rev. and Mrs. Sprague were missionaries of the
National Spiritualist Association for thirteen consecutive
years, holding meetings in thirty-two different states of
our Union. They organized and chartered 210 Spiritualist

Mrs. Clarissa Adelia Sprague

churches, and three state auxiliaries to the National Spiritualist Association.

They traveled together in the work forty-eight years. Mrs. Sprague passed to spirit life February 6, 1929.

# THE SCIENCE OF MAGNETIC, MENTAL AND SPIRITUAL HEALING, WITH INSTRUCTIONS HOW TO HEAL BY LAYING ON OF HANDS

*by*

## REV. E. W. SPRAGUE

The author is a minister of the Gospel of Spiritualism, of forty-nine years experience as a platform, test and message medium, also the author of many books on the subject of Spiritualism.

# INDEX

Magnetic, Mental and Spiritual healing is a Science which has been revealed to Spiritualists by the spirits of their loved ones, together with the proper method of its application. It becomes my privilege in this work to publish these facts for the benefit of all who are suffering from the effects of ill health and for the instruction of all who wish to learn of its wonderful power and also for those who wish to develop it properly, and to such workers as want to "Add to their faith knowledge" as mentioned by 2nd Peter, 1 Chap., 5th verse.

The author has had more than fifty years of experience with the subject of Magnetic, Mental and Spiritual healing. His faithful partner in life, Mrs. Clarissa Adelia Sprague, his wife, with whom he spent 61 years of happiness, before she passed to the higher life, was one who healed by laying on of hands—by spirit power; and we needed no other physician and seldom employed one because we did not need their services. Let no one misunderstand. We believe in medicine and medical doctors, but Mrs. Sprague's mediumship saved the family from needing any other doctor and we can truly say there is virtue in nearly all methods of healing, but gladly state that there is no healing power that we have discovered that is so wonderful, so pleasantly applied, and so thoroughly effectual or so easily developed, as Magnetic, Mental and Spiritual healing, by laying on of hands.

The mind controls the body. A thought may paralize the nerves. Through thought of fear the heart may cease to beat. A thought of exultation may quicken the heart's action. The heart responds to the thought of good or evil, joy or sorrow, pain or pleasure, etc., as does the mind.

The laws of attraction and repulsion with human beings are governed and controlled largely by the power of mind, and two minds, that of healer and patient, may harmonize and get good results, or antagonize and destroy conditions, breeding inharmony which spoils conditions for spirits to operate.

"In the effort to do good one cultivates his own soul. In the cultivation of soul, one develops health." Soul culture generates health and happiness. We should get these facts well established in our minds.

### WEBSTER'S DEFINITION OF THE WORD INFECTIOUS

"Infectious: Capable of being easily diffused or spread; sympathetic; readily communicated; as infectious mirth." This is the sense in which this word is used throughout this book.

### OUR WONDERFUL PHYSICAL BODIES

The human body is a wonderful and intricate machine. It is self-lubricating. It oils every place where there is friction and manufactures and furnishes its own oil. It is a self-regulating machine built somewhat on the plan of perpetual motion. It is perpetual emotion in performing its various functions, as long as it is inhabited by its spirit owner. It works continually whether the spirit is sleeping or waking, and the emotions are always ready and alert to respond to any condition with which they come in contact. The human organism is a veritable factory and self-repair shop. If by accident a bone is broken, it goes right to work to mend it. If the outer covering, the cuticle, is by accident cut away, it goes right to work and manufactures new skin to cover the naked flesh that protects the nervous system.

If a limb is severed, this wise and wonderful machine mechanically heals over the exposed parts. If a small vein is punctured and blood is running away, it has a fashion of mechanically congealing the blood and stopping its flow. If food in the stomach is undigested, it gets rid of it, acting intelligently, or as though it knew the necessity of so doing.

Its prerogative is self-cure. It is always using the self-generated natural forces to restore and retain the health of its own organism. It is a self-building and self-restoring machine. It manufactures and prepares the chemical materials and forces necessary to build and keep itself in repair and if properly cared for, and not interfered with by too great obstructing conditions, it will keep itself in good order until its machinery is entirely worn out. It manufactures saliva, gastric juices, chyle, chyme, all the other products used in the manufacture and repairing of the whole structure. It is really a manufacturing chemist, with powers so intricate as to appear almost miraculous. Each one of us is possessed of one of these beautiful organisms and we should be grateful to our Creator for it. We should also show our appreciation of it by using it properly and by taking the very best of care of it.

We have only to make the conditions nature demands to accomplish any natural result. Cause and effect are the inexorable laws of nature. The more pure and refined one becomes the greater will be his powers which clearly explains the fact that the better life we live, the better healer or medium for any phase we may become.

The elements of nature used to heal oneself are the same elements of electro-magnetic vital forces that the healer uses to heal his patients. Magnetic, Mental and Spiritual healing is not a miracle, and never was. It is a science operating under the power of natural law. And Modern Spiritualism revealed this fact to the world, and it shall have the credit of having done it. All the world shall know this truth in time.

Prayers for the sick are potent factors in healing if the patient has faith in prayer. His faith places him in a receptive mood and causes him to absorb the forces. Often Jesus is reported as teaching that the patient must have faith and He berated them saying: "O, ye of little Faith." When He went home to see His mother and sisters He tried to convince the people of His mesiahship or mediumship, but He said He "could do no great miracle among them because of their unbelief."

Jesus said repeatedly "Thy faith hath made thee whole." See Matt. IX, 22; Mark V, 34; Mark X, 52; Luke VIII, 48; Luke XVII, 19.

Many, many passages of Scripture similar to these quoted, could be mentioned showing that Jesus was a mental healer as well as a magnetic healer, who like Modern Spiritualistic healers, healed by laying on of hands.

## SPIRITUAL HEALING

Every mortal is a spirit whether inhabiting

the physical body in which we find ourselves here to-day, or whether within the spiritual body in the world beyond the grave.

Spirit is behind every movement or manifestation men produce. It is our spirit that sees, that hears, that speaks, when we see, hear, or speak. It is our spirit that moves our foot or hand. It is our spirit that does our thinking. The spirit is the moving power behind every manifestation we produce, therefore each such manifestation is truly a spirit manifestation.

In plain magnetic healing alone there may be no other spirit manipulating the vital forces of the healer excepting the healer's own spirit. In spiritual healing the spirit helpers who operate through the healer's mediumship, apply the spiritual elements or spiritualizing the elements of vital force furnished by the magnetic healer, thus stimulating the physical, mental and the spiritual forces of the patient, harmonizing and equalizing them into normal action, and when normal action is accomplished the patient is placed in an entirely healthful condition and is normal in every way.

Healing the sick brings happiness
To those who suffer pain,
It fills one who heals with gladness
That words can scarce explain.
To relieve distress and sorrow
While knowing as some do
That the force and power they borrow
From angels good and true.
Is a blessed consolation,
Filling with joyous pride,
A wonderful revelation
That with us does abide.

### MAN A MAGNET

Man is a magnet. He generates magnetism, imbues it with vitality, applies it to the working parts of his physical organs and keeps them going from year to year. Some men generate much more magnetism and vital force than they need for their own use and the residue is thrown off, and often goes to waste when it could be used to heal the sick and supply those who are lacking in vitality.

## MENTAL HEALING

The mind of man is a great power. The Scripture says: "As he thinketh in his heart so is he" (Prov. XXIII, 7). If one thinks he is sick and believes it, the thinking it, will make him sick. If he thinks he is well and feels it down deep in his mind, and lives the natural life, he must be well. If he thinks evil, evil will come to him. If he thinks good, things will appear good to him. It is the law, and everything is governed by law. What we send out returns to us.

## SPIRITUAL HEALING

The fact is that thinking along spiritual lines generates healthful forces and furnishes healthful conditions. Thinking spiritually is harmonious mental action, and mental harmony is an important element of good health. Spirituality is harmonious always and harmony generates good health.

The spirit friends live in harmony and generate spiritual forces and live in a spiritual atmosphere similar to the magnetism of mortals, but much more harmonious and spiritual and they bring their forces and apply them to the patient through the healer with his healing forces, and with the patient's forces also, if he is susceptible to spirit influence, which makes the healing power doubly strong. Then there are spirit chemists with some healers who can discern the lack of any element in a patient's system, and can and do supply that needed element and the patient is healed.

This kind of healing, when conditions are good, eliminates poisons from the system of the patient, supplies vital forces to strengthen and place in normal action the weak organs of the patient. Healing by laying on of hands when understood and properly applied is the most potent method of healing. How often does one hear of a case of instantaneous cure of the sick by the use of drugs? There are cases occurring constantly where one treatment by laying on of hands cures the patient. Beginners should keep this fact in mind.

Men and women are magnets generating vital forces and may impart them to each other, through the application of the magnetic, mental and spiritual powers with which they are endowed by nature. The mind and will has wonderful power over the body. Good thoughts produce good health. Evil thoughts generate ill health.

### MANY POSSESS HEALING POWERS

Many people are natural healers and with the understanding of this fact and study of the subject may develop to do much good to suffering humanity.

Healing by laying on of hands is a natural science, and when this becomes known to the world and the false teachings of the orthodox Christian church that it is or was a miracle, in the time of Jesus and His apostles, it will then be taught and practiced by the schools of medicine as a natural science. Christianity has, by calling it a miracle, kept the world from investigating and learning this natural scientific truth.

One purpose of this book is to help people to understand healing, and to teach them how to develop it, and use it, by laying on of hands. There may be one or more in every family who can heal the rest of them, and this work will teach those who are healers, how to develop and practice it.

## MAN A MAGNET

The emanations from the human body are called magnetism — electro-magnetic emanations. These emanations form a miniature photosphere and have a circulation.

This magnetic aura contains the impress and records of the conditions of the body and of the mind from which it radiates. And through the use of this wonderful, invisible, physical emanation, the phenomena of mediumship in all its phases, including Magnetic, Mental and Spiritual healing are produced by the spirit operators clothed in flesh, with the aid of those in spirit life.

The records of the state of the body and the condition of the mind of the one from whom these emanations radiate are impressed upon these auras; and a medium who is developed for this phase—and there are many who are— can, with the aid of their spirit helpers see their state of health, general characteristics, condition of mind, etc., and give them much good advice, instruction, and help. And the healer besides diagnosing their disease can heal their infirmities by laying on of hands. These are real blessings.

Modern Spiritualism is enlightening the world on these all-important truths. Some phenomena termed miracles by Christians as taught in the Scriptures, Spiritualism demonstrates to be natural phenomena, and they are occurring to-day in every civilized country on earth and Spiritualism explains the necessary conditions and laws governing them.

We are all human magnets generating magnetism and vitalizing it with oxygen by breathing air into the lungs where the blood takes it and distributes it to every part of the body.

### WE CALL IT GOD, BUT KNOW NO MORE

Who made the forms we mortals wear?
    We do not know.
There's nothing with them can compare,
    It's truly so.
Its wonders our deep thoughts enhance,
We can't believe they came by chance;
Who planned these forms that we adore?
We call it God, but know no more.

Our hearts that beat from year to year,
  We know not why.
The cause to us does not appear,
  But by-and-by,
When heart-beats cease, we cannot stay,
Instantly we are called away.
Who planned that all must leave this shore?
We call it God, but know no more.

How does a mortal learn to think?
  How can we know?
It may be said it is instinct,
  But is it so?
But instinct has an unknown source,
Which leaves us in the dark, of course.
And just as we have said before,
We call it God and know no more.

When we are called we must away.
  Indeed it's so.
Who calls us and who names the day
  That we must go?
All life is one great mystery,
And every day makes history.
First birth, then death. This life is o'er,
We say God called and know no more.

We leave behind all we possess,
  When stops our heart.
Including pain and sore distress
  When we depart.
With perfect forms that mortals wear
All other forms do not compare.
Leaving our all for-ever-more
To God above, yet know no more.

Parting with all causes distress,
  But it must be.
Later it brings great happiness,
  When we are free.
Spirit forms to all are given.
All, when earned, inherit heaven.
The time may come on yonder shore
When we, of God, learn something more.

### EVERY FACULTY OF THE MIND OR ORGAN OF THE BODY IS A SERVANT OF THE SPIRIT WITHIN

One should treat his body and mind well always, never overworking or under-exercising either. Some persons are in good health while others have poor health in the same climate. Change them to some other climate and the sick ones may regain their good health and the others may become sick. This may be because of the different temperaments; and the state of mind largely caused· by the change in environment, associations, etc. The healthy one not finding congenial surroundings, becomes dissatisfied, lapses into a state of mind, causing ill health, while those who were ill finding congenial conditions in the new environment or location, were placed in a happy state of mind, which was all that was needed to eliminate the elements of disease and build up his physical health.

Congenial associations place the mind in the right condition to draw to one the generative forces of the universe that produce good health, So it may be seen that it is not always the change of climate that heals so much as it is the condition of mind. A contented mind and a happy disposition are powerful therapeutics.

One may develop will-power to overcome adverse conditions, and mental qualities will lift him above many detrimental experiences, until he may become immune to adverse environments and their influence; enjoying mental freedom, good health and all the other requisites to happiness. All this he may possess through acquiring a thorough knowledge of Spiritual Science and applying such knowledge in his daily life.

Many persons, knowing how to proceed in the matter, may become centers from which may flow through the psychic ether these forces that convey to others physical health and mental poise.

The body registers mental impressions, be they of the happy or unhappy kind, joy or sorrow, health or sickness, love or hate, hope or despair, etc., and every such impression carries with it an influence of vigor or lassitude, strength or weakness, health or sickness.

Nature through her own scientific processes heals every disease when proper conditions are made; conditions that are in conformity to her laws. The true physician is the one who studies and applies nature's laws, uses natural methods; and what is needed most is a knowledge of these laws and forces; they are very potent and will prove almost omnipotent when we understand them thoroughly. Their greatest power lies outside the physical realm. The study of the mental and the spiritual is revealing these mighty forces and blessing the world more and more as their truths are discovered and applied.

### PHYSICAL CONDITIONS RESPOND TO MENTAL IMPRESSIONS

We may hypnotize ourselves with the suggestion that we are sick and through that suggestion become invalids. Fortunately the law works both ways and we may by auto-suggestion hypnotize ourselves with the thought of health and through it, become well and healthy and with the proper application of natural law from the spirit and mortal sides of life, we should continue in the best of health to a very great old age and pass on to spirit life without a pain.

### MAGNETISM IS OF THE SPIRIT

"From the facts demonstrated by spiritual science the higher philosophy is deduced."

The magnetic forces are of the spirit and to understand them is to understand much of the phenomena of everyday life that is otherwise not understood. Acquaintance with these forces and the laws controlling them makes clear the naturalness of the phenomena of the seance room.

Man is a magnet and generates or gathers these spiritual forces from the unseen. These occult forces (secret or hidden) are the propelling power of mind and matter. Our magnetism contains the vital principles of physical life and is used to produce any and every manifestation of man, whether physical, mental, spiritual, or psychical. Live magnetism is permeated with the spirit influence of mortals. It is a material substance, perhaps a fluid.

All phases of spirit phenomena are produced through magnetic and vital forces of mortals. All phenomena are produced by certain rates of vibration, and where one is attuned magnetically to the proper vibration for the production of any one of the many phases of mediumship, that one may be used by the spirits to produce such phase of the phenomena. This fact includes the phase of healing by laying on of hands or magnetic and spiritual healing.

A Buffalo, New York, physician wrote as follows: "I believe that plant life contains elements and remedial agents for the cure of every disease to which mankind is subject." Medical men know that plant life generates elements that act upon the diseased organs of the human body, and bring relief from pain and suffering. Certain roots, herbs, and barks stimulate the action of the heart and other organs and this physician's idea is probably correct.

## MAN THE HUMAN PLANT

A human being in good health generates all the elements used in the development, growth, sustenance and operation of all the parts and organs of the human body, and some people generate more, much more, of these elements than are used in supplying their own bodies and are constantly throwing off those elements of vital force that produce health. Such people if they are of the proper temperament, of a congenial and sympathetic nature, make excellent healers. Healers generating less of these elements may receive more of the spiritual forces.

A person of low vitality is more liable to take contagious diseases than one in good health, because the one in good health throws out his magnetic aura and keeps the diseased aura away, while the person of low vitality absorbs the diseased auras of the contagion.

This fact applies in magnetic and spiritual healing. The patient being in a low state of vitality absorbs the healer's healthful auras as quickly as the diseased auras and this health-ladened aura of the healer is absorbed by the patient and stimulates the diseased organs to new activity and convalescence follows as a natural result.

### THERE ARE NO MIRACLES

Magnetic and Spiritual healing is not miraculous as is taught by Christianity. It is a natural fact, and is accomplished under natural law. A miracle, to occur at all, must transcend the laws of the universe, therefore there are no miracles; there can be no miracles. Everything is governed by law. Cause and effect are dominant throughout the universe. Magnetic and Spiritual healing is natural and scientific and the laws governing are well explained by the philosophy of Modern. Spiritualism, and these laws are as well understood by well-informed Spiritualists as any other facts in nature are understood by other men of material science. This book makes clear this natural science.

Magnetic and Spiritual healing is a scientifically demonstrated fact and Modern Spiritualism must be credited with having brought that fact to light. The spirits returning and communicating have revealed the proper methods, the mode of operations, etc., showing that it is accomplished through processes of natural law. This of course contradicts the teaching of the Christian church which makes and holds the claim that the Magnetic and Spiritual healings recorded in the Christian Bible were miracles wrought by Almighty God through his prophets. The skeptic may ask: "Why did not God continue his prophets down to the present day? There seems to be great need of them, since the world is growing more and more doubtful of the Christian creeds." And while the Christian church is trying to study up an answer to the question, we will let Spiritualism answer it briefly and truly. Spiritualism says: *The prophets are continued down to the present day,* and hundreds of thousands of good Christians have learned this fact, and are visiting daily these modern prophets, attending their public meetings and seances and are having private readings with them. Thousands of good Christians are being healed of their diseases by the power of spirits acting through these modern prophets (spirit mediums). In fact there are more people of the Christian church among those who are patients of these Spiritualistic healers than of any other class of people as Christians are in the majority as a class of believers in spiritual healing.

### MAGNETISM OF HUMAN BEINGS

The laws of nature are perfection and infallible in their every manifestation, when viewed from the standpoint of reason, and many thinkers worship at nature's shrine. From the spirit side of life where a clearer vision prevails, these wonders are multiplied to the highly developed spirits, almost infinitely. Oh, the wonderful perfection in the action of natural law! The more we know of it and the better application we make of it in this life, the better children will be born; the more years we will live in this life; the better health will be ours; the more we will know of life here and hereafter; and the better we will be prepared to enter that life. Modern Spiritualism is teaching the world many of nature's Spiritual laws and instructing us how to utilize them in the unfoldment of the higher faculties of mankind.

One of the greatest of these faculties is that of Spirit Mediumship which consists of many phases, among which is the one of Magnetic and Spiritual healing as shown by the teachings of this book. It is revealed to many and will be to unnumbered others who seek to know, that the enveloping atmosphere of human beings is composed of electro-magnetic and vital forces which constitute the battery through which the more than forty phases of spirit mediumship are produced; and that these auras are permeated with the impressions of the thoughts of its generators. This aura contains the record of its owner's state of health which the spiritual healer may read and understand.

## MEDIUMS TAKE CONDITIONS

Many personating mediums, as they become enveloped in the patient's magnetic aura, take on his condition and feelings, thus locating his trouble; and applying the healing forces to the diseased parts, producing normal action thereof.

## MORTALS ARE SPIRITS—THIS THE SPIRIT WORLD

We mortals are all spirits, now living in one sphere or section of the spirit world. Every manifestation that we produce whether of the physical or the mental is a spirit manifestation, a manifestation produced by our spirits, and any act or thought produced by us is as impossible of explanation as any phenomena of Spiritualism. No one knows how he moves his hand or foot, how he controls his vocal organs to speak. No one can explain his process of thinking because no one knows how he thinks. One only knows that he thinks and that he cannot stop thinking as long as he is alive and in good health. No great scientist has thus far been able to tell how one snaps his finger, shuts his eye, or produces any manifestation. Yet some truly innocent people think, because we Spiritualists do not clearly explain the phenomena of the seance room to their comprehension that it is fraud and trickery, while others not well informed regarding the philosophy of the phenomena of Spiritualism, yet have become convinced of the fact that they do occur, consider them miracles, when the fact is they are neither fraud nor miracles, but are genuine and natural phenomena.

We mortals are liable to demand too much at times, but when we consider the many things we do not comprehend we may listen to what Rev. John Wesley, the founder of Methodism, said regarding spirit manifestations in his time. He said: "It is true there are several of them (spirit phenomena) which I do not comprehend, but this is with me a very slender objection, for what is it which I do comprehend, even of the things I see daily? Truly not the smallest grain of sand, or spire of grass. I know not how the one grows or how particles of the other cohere together. What pretense have I then to deny well-attested facts because I cannot comprehend them."* "But whoever are pleased or displeased, I must testify what I believe to be the truth."

Rev. John Wesley believed in spirit return and wanted to retain it in the Methodist creed, and greatly opposed those who were not in favor of it. Rev. John Wesley visited trance mediums according to his own statement as recorded in the life of Wesley before the year 1808, but it was cut out of later editions.

### HUMAN BEINGS GENERATE MAGNETISM

There is a magnetic aura surrounding all persons that they generate and are constantly throwing off. With some persons this aura is more electric than with others. This is shown as electric sparkles or crackles fly from a steel comb passing through the hair; or by rubbing one's feet on a Wilton carpet and touching one's finger against the bare flesh of another, causing a shock or pricking sensation, and by holding one's finger ends close to a swift run-

*See "News From the Invisible World" from the pen of Rev. John Wesley, for more of Wesley's Spiritualism republished by Rev. E. W. Sprague.

ning belt driving machinery, where it is partially dark, which shows the lighted aura as it flies from the finger ends. This is shown in many other ways. A very sensitive person can sense the difference in a largely magnetic person and one who is strongly electric.

The magnetism of individuals differ as much as their personal appearance differs. This fact I have tested thoroughly all the years of my mediumistic work.

This magnetism of mortals, this aura, is permeated with the condition of mind and body of its owner and reveals his state of health, likes and dislikes. His very thoughts are stamped upon every circulating atom of this aura as they are stamped upon his features, and spirits can and do read the character and give many proofs of this fact and transmit them to their mediums.

CLAIRVOYANTS DISCERN DISEASE AND LOCATE IT

Clairvoyant healers discern the disease of the patient, learn the cause of it, watch the results of their treatments upon the diseased organs, etc. Well-developed clairvoyant healers can look through the patient's organism like looking through a glass bottle, and can see the action of the different organs. I have known many such clairvoyants; there were three of them in our family, and I now am going to tell my readers who they were because some of them may doubt my authority for this statement. One of these mediums was my brother Franklin, one was my blessed wife (now in spirit life) and the other was the writer of this book. My brother and my wife could heal sick people. I could not heal the sick, because I took on the conditions of the patient, and it was hard to throw it off. All three of us could see, feel, and locate the disease of the patient.

Oh, what a pity that the medical fraternity do not study and learn what this Magnetic, Mental and Spiritual healing consists of; and when understood practice it with the aid of such healers, and also teach it in their medical schools, and freely give the people of the world the benefit of this God-given method of curing the sick and relieving them of their suffering. This is done in the same manner and by the same methods as those employed by Jesus of

Nazareth, His apostles and disciples, namely: by laying on of hands, which is fully explained in this work.

There is a better understanding of the subject today than ever before. It is as truly a science as any other medical science. Healing by laying on of hands is a great truth and is proven and successfully demonstrated. Magnetic, Mental, and Spiritual healing is being practiced by Spiritualists in every civilized country in the world today, and somewhat by Christians. Modern Spiritualism is introducing Christianity to Christ's method of healing the sick, as is shown in the acceptance and advocacy of the Episcopal Church in what they have named Emmanuelism and as many other Christian denominations are adopting it and practicing it in their churches in different parts of the country under different names as *"Faith Healing," "Christian Healing,"* etc.

## ANIMAL MAGNETISM
### A FUNDAMENTAL PRINCIPLE OF LIFE

Man is at the head of all the animal creation and generates the finest, most powerful aura permeated with his higher propelling mental forces, and it contains the vital principles of physical life and is used in every manifestation produced by man and by spirits through mediums whether the manifestations are physical, mental, or spiritual.

The Magnetic, Mental and Spiritual healer, when he places his hands, or mind, or both, upon a patient who is suffering pain, simply creates a harmonious vibration, temporarily or permanently, all of which is dependent upon conditions. If but partially restored to health, more treatments may be necessary, but if the normal condition is permanently restored, the patient is healed and nature takes care of the case again until the violation of her laws brings on a return of illness. A patient may be permanently healed with one treatment or it may take time and more treatments, all depends upon the nature of the disease, and the conditions which the healer and patient furnish.

### DANGER IS AVOIDED BY HEALING MAGNETICALLY

A healer cannot overload his patient with his magnetism, because when the patient is filled with it, he will not absorb any more. He may take too much of certain kinds of medicine, or the wrong medicine may be given him, as is sometimes the case; but this danger is almost entirely avoided in magnetic, mental and spiritual healing.

## MAGNETISM IS A LIVING PRINCIPLE OF LIFE AND HAS GREAT HEALING POWER

Magnetism is a material substance seen by clairvoyants but not visible to the physical eye through the microscope, and like electricity it may be a fluid. It is a human emanation of sublimated, rarified, etherialized matter in motion, moving in circles when not obstructed, and is acted upon, moved and manipulated by the power of mind of its owner.

Its rotary motion may be increased by the thoughts and the emotions of the mind.

## PROPER METHOD OF MANIPULATION

In healing the patient one should place the right hand upon the forehead and the left hand upon the back of the neck and head. The right hand being positive throws out the magnetism and the left hand negative receives the magnetism as it circulates in circles passing from the healer's right hand through the patient's brain, magnetizing it and charging the patient's entire nervous system with his electromagnetic vitality. When the patient's system is fully charged (the time it takes to charge it depends upon the patient's receptivity) then the healer should manipulate the patient all over from head to foot in many cases, throwing off the infected magnetism of the patient, and snapping it off the finger ends, as shown in Figure No. 3. In throwing off this diseased aura the healer should always be careful not to draw it to or toward the vital organs, but to throw it aside.

After throwing off freely, he should apply his forces to the patient by rubbing, tapping, gently slapping, kneading, stroking, or rubbing the surface swiftly, causing friction.

*Magnetic friction* is one of the finest treatments. It creates action, stimulates the system, reviving the circulation of the blood, drawing it to the surface and aids in bringing into normal activity the whole system.

Beating drives the magnetism in and draws

the blood to the surface, aiding circulation. Not all cases can be thus treated. All depends upon the kind of disease, the condition of the patient, etc. The healer is usually impressed concerning the best way to manipulate each case.

### SPIRITUAL HEALING

Our spirit friends generate a spiritual magnetism all their own. Mediums feel and understand its power. It is more potent than the magnetism of men in the mortal, because it is more refined and pure.

The magnetic forces generated by spirit and mortal constitute the intermediary between spirit and matter. It is used to convey the message of men and spirits between the visible and the invisible realms, as electricity is used in wireless telegraphy to send man's message across the mighty ocean. It is used to connect the spirit of man in this life with his own body, as it is in every other instance when matter is animated with life.

Spirit chemists through certain mediums may discern the condition of a patient, note a superfluity or a lack of certain elements in his body, and through the medium's forces may eliminate them or supply such elements as are needed, and instantaneous healing is accomplished. Everything depends upon conditions.

Where conditions are not good the process of healing is retarded, and in such cases it often takes time to heal a patient. Conditions permitting, the patient may be healed instantly. "Magnetic and Spiritual Healing" embodies what good there is in "Faith Cure," "Prayer Cure," "Mental Healing," "Divine Healing," and every other legitimate method of mental and spiritual healing known, including "Emmanuelism," "Suggestive Therapeutics," etc. In fact Spiritual Healing was made clear by Modern Spiritualism and it is the mother of all the New Thought Methods. It teaches the laws governing these forces and instructs us in their application. Not a single new thought along these lines of healing, so far as we know, has yet been presented that is of the least value whatever, that was not previously given to the world by Modern Spiritualism in its philosophy and facts of Spiritual Science. It explains scientifically the so-called "Miraculous" healing of the sick by Jesus and his Apostles.

There is virtue in most methods of healing, but Spiritual healing stands preeminent, and may be used to great advantage by all. Many people are mediums for this phase, and in some it may be easily developed.

### THE HUMAN ORGANISM A DYNAMO

The human organism is a veritable electro-magnetic dynamo, generating vital forces of a nature essential to the production and preservation of the good health of the organism in which it is generated. These electro-magnetic forces may be generated in an organism to that degree that they are not all needed nor all used in vitalizing the system. In such cases there is a constant overflow of these forces that are cast off from the human dynamo. This overflow of vital forces may easily be applied to other organisms that are lacking in them and through such application, by the laying on of hands, they are supplied and the patient made vigorous and healthy.

### SPIRITUAL DYNAMICS

(Dynamics, a dynamic force; a motive

power. Dyna, a prefix denoting power — Webster.)

Spiritual healing is accomplished through the application of the spirit forces through the instrumentality of the medium. The medium being receptive to the influence of the spirit is charged with the electro-magnetic forces of the spirit and applies them to the patient in the same manner as he does the magnetism generated by himself. The spiritual forces are much more powerful than the forces of a person in the mortal. They are blended with them by the will of the spirit healer and the acquiescence of the mortal healer and by the desire of the patient.

The spirit guide may be a spirit chemist and able to analyze the patient's condition physically, mentally, morally, and spiritually, and if the patient is physically ill, he supplies the spiritual forces and the elements needed when found in the vital forces of the medium or of the circles. If the patient is mentally ill, he supplies the mental forces necessary to his recovery. If morally unbalanced or spiritually weak, the spirit furnishes the spiritual elements needed to help the patient to regain his mental, moral and spiritual equilibrium thus harmonizing the complete man.

Through this method of treatment the patient's spiritual powers of mediumship is often developed.

### APPLICATION OF THIS HEALING EASY AND EFFECTUAL

The application of this vital force to the receptive patient is easier to accomplish and often has fully as great or greater effect than the transfusion of blood; both are very valuable remedies.

### SPIRITUAL SCIENCE, PSYCHIC LAW USED IN HEALING THE SICK

Chiropractic adjustments, osteopathic treatments, magnetic healing, mental therapeutics and spiritual healing constitute a most complete system of healing. Proper chiropractic adjustments and osteopathic treatments place the bony and muscular structure of the patient in their normal condition. Magnetic treatments, vitalize the nervous system and place the organs of the body in normal working order. Mental therapeutics places the dictator in control of his physical system.

Spiritual healing awakens the patient's spiritual nature and prepares him for the reception of the spiritual forces and elements that quicken the vibrations of the entire combination, physical, mental and spiritual. There is nothing of value taught in "Science of mental healing," "Christian Science," "Divine Science," "Emmanuelism," or any of the other "New Thought" methods of healing, that has not been and now is taught in Spiritual Science, or Psychic Science of Modern Spiritualism, where all of value taught by them originated.

### SELF-HEALING, USING AUTO-SUGGESTION AND WILL-POWER

By the use of one's will-power, one may send his vital forces to any part of the body. He may imbue those forces with his thoughts of healing and set in operation the magnetic auras and vital fluids of the physical organism, causing them to act upon any organ he may wish to strengthen. He may strengthen and imbue these forces with great power and stimulate the organs to greater activity by applying his thoughts of healing and pushing them into action, by the use of his will, though this requires practice to develop.

By the vigorous action of the mind one may stimulate the vital action of his own forces and thus through auto-suggestion, self-suggestion, he may heal himself or at least assist the healer in curing him. The patient should use his kindly aid when being healed.

If any organ of one's body is sluggish or inactive, a greater supply of vital force may be forwarded to that organ and made to do duty in stimulating it into greater and more normal action, and when normal action of the organs is secured, good health is the result, because the normal action of all the organs is good health.

### HOW TO INCREASE THE ACTIVITY OF A SLUGGISH ORGAN OF THE BODY

Go to your quiet room where no one will be likely to divert your attention from the subject of your treatment. Lie down on your back with arms extended for a few minutes, relaxing every muscle, then place your right hand (which is positive, if you are right handed), on the sluggish organ you wish to revive. Place your mind on the organ, viewing it minutely in its construction, noting every peculiarity of its make-up, including especially the circulation of blood through it. Then with your will send the blood rushing through it, clearing it of all obstructions. If it is inflamed and you send a current of your vital force through it you may revive its activities and cause it to function properly. Do this often until cured. The practice of this develops the power to do it, just as the use of the blacksmith's arm develops his muscle. If one is left handed, the left hand is positive and the right hand the negative, and the left hand should be placed on the forehead and the right on the back of the neck at the base of the brain, to charge the system of the patient.

### A SCHOOL FOR SPIRITUAL HEALERS

Modern Spiritualism very much needs a school of Magnetic, Mental, and Spiritual healing, where healers by laying on of hands can go and learn how to use this mighty healing power.

Every healer should study anatomy and seek to develop his clairvoyance so as to be able to look within the patient and see the effect of his treatment upon the patient's organs. It is true that many spiritual healers have that power now, but a school of that kind could be made of great assistance to many of our healers, and would place Magnetic and Spiritual healing before the public in its natural scientific and true light, and would become a still greater blessing to the world's sick and suffering people, and also would advance the cause of Spiritualism. If I were able I would gladly endow a school of this kind. I hope some good soul may see this great need, and endow the Morris Pratt Institute of Whitewater, Wisconsin, with such an addition to its present splendid line of spiritual education. Such a school would surely be well patronized and would be a great help to the Institute.

### THE NERVOUS SYSTEM

The body can be thought of as a mass of very fine wires called nerves from which all parts of the body are brought into harmony.

The brain controls the reasoning process, but we have mechanical movements which never reach the brain.

When a motion has once been learned the brain ceases to function and we think of the act as mechanical because the nerves used only go as far as the spinal cord and back to the muscles. They do not go to the brain. However, the mind has influence over the entire system and affects more or less the functions of the various organs. For instance, anger causes deep breathing and increases the heart action. Fear may paralyze a nerve, stop the heart beating, and cause death. The state of one's mind has great influence over the body. Happiness of mind produces health. Despondency causes sickness. These are well-known facts and should teach everyone to think good and happy thoughts and to avoid thoughts of fear, thoughts of evil, and to be cheerful and will themselves to enjoy life, seeking the good in everything and in everybody.

The wrong doer has lost his way and needs our sympathy and aid in finding it again. Oh, how much the world needs this education.

The solar plexus lies behind the stomach and may be considered as a local switchboard, connected with an electrical telephone system. It is a group of nerves and branches of nerves that are connected with the vital organs such as the stomach, heart and kidneys. The solar plexus is sometimes called the abdominal brain.

The solar plexus belongs to the sympathetic group of nerves which are supposed not to be directly controlled by the mind; for instance, it is not possible to stop the heart beating or to stop the lungs entirely from inhaling breath and exhaling it, by merely thinking about it, but the action of the emotions will retard or accelerate the heart-beats. Fear, or undue emotion, will retard digestion. The state of mind often rules the emotions. It may govern and control them in some measure.

The spirit in control of the mind and will has power over the entire system and by placing his hands upon an organ of the body that is not performing its full function may by manipulation and willing it determinedly, send the vital energy of the system to that organ and strengthen it to continue its work normally. Of course the spirit may not be able to accomplish this the first time he tries, but the power is easily developed in many people, but not everyone can do it.

It is easily proven that vital forces may be collected from some parts of the system and sent out of the medium's finger ends into a patient's system to strengthen and increase the power of the organs of the patient. Chemical, physical, electro-magnetism is generated by nerve cells in different parts of the body, but especially so in the spinal ganglion on either side of the spinal cord. That is one reason why chills chase up and down the spine of the medium when the spirit applies his spirit forces to the nervous system at the base of the brain, as is explained on page 65. These spinal ganglions generate currents of vitality that are used in moving muscles and the like.

Now, I am a spirit in control of my system and can draw this vital force to my hands and use it to open and shut them as pleases my mind. Why can I not send these vital forces out of my finger ends for a sick man to absorb and use to build up his depleted body? This is what healing by laying on of hands does. Magnetic, Mental and Spiritual healing is a healng science.

The solar plexus contains a large branching group of nerves and as it fulfils the laws of conduction in conducting the vital forces to the vital organs of the body it becomes the ideal place to apply the healing forces one would naturally think, for a general treatment of the entire system. Though it is better to apply the treatment directly to the diseased organ after the system has been charged, as explained on page 70.

### SPIRITS UTILIZING THE BRAIN

The brain is a veritable electric switchboard. It is the central station of the electro-magnetic system, the nerves and muscles of which are charged with this vital force and the spirit is its operator. He lives here. He possesses a mind and will. If he makes up his mind to do something and wills the body to do it, he applies the vital forces to muscles and causes them to act in obedience to his will. If he says,

"Let's go," he applies the vital forces to the muscles of the legs and they are at once brought into action. If he changes his mind and decides to return, he turns his body around and starts it on its way back. He can only do this by using the vital forces generated in these nerve cells and he is the supreme ruler of his system. He may rule it wisely or unwisely.

The more we know about our wonderful bodies, its organs and their requirements, the better care we will be able to take of the entire system. This fact is important because good care of the body keeps it in good working order and good health is the natural result.

### TREATING CERTAIN DISEASES

In treating a patient it is well to have a chair that turns back forming a padded table on which the healer may get at any part of the patient's body easily, and the patient can rest at ease, and relax every muscle and let go of every nerve, as he would in normal health when trying to go to sleep.

Disease caused by nervousness, or nervousness caused by disease is easily overcome by the healer laying on of hands when the patient's mind is right, and he is in harmonious sympathy with the healer, and has faith in his ability to heal.

Extreme pain is often caused by congestion, resulting from inflammation which retards the circulation of the blood. The healer may increase the flow of the blood after he has charged the patient's nervous system, by placing his hands over the congested parts, and magnetizing them, then by swift and long strokes and also by strokes of friction, produced on the skin by short, swift, downward strokes, with the healer's mind determined to increase the blood circulation. If the healer is strong and the conditions good the inflammation may be swept away and the congestion with it, as the rise in the river carries away the flood trash lodged in the eddies along the shore. Magnetic, Mental and Spiritual healing is as natural as the sunshine, or rainfall. It is not miraculous, as taught by the Christian church.

When a patient is not susceptible to the healing forces, or when the case needs quick relief, rubbing, tapping, slapping or lively manipulation of the skin and muscles may be necessary. The well-developed healer will be impressed in each case how best to manipulate it.

### HEALING METHODS ILLUSTRATED

The following eight illustrations show the mode of operation of the magnetism generated by men and the application of the spirit forces to the healing medium when treating a patient.

The sensitive person feels almost pushed away, and turning away feels he does not like that person, yet he knows nothing against him, and will not seek his company. This is no condition for successful healing and little else that requires confidence and harmony.

Such people are very liable to antagonize each other, and may sometimes become real enemies. However, when they understand this truth, and the power of mind over their magnetic auras, and both apply that power properly, harmoniously, but determinedly, they may overcome that condition so that their auras will freely blend. This often occurs where people have to be closely associated in business, and in other close relations. Resolves of mind to overcome the antipathy toward each other cause the auras to break and blend at times and the former opponents understand each other and become friends.

Figure 1

Figure 1 shows two persons whose magnetic auras do not blend. Dr. Andrew Jackson Davis explains that when auras come together and do not blend their action is like two rubber balls being pushed against each other.

Figure 2

Figure 2 illustrates two persons coming together whose circles of magnetism break and blend and the circulation surrounds them both. These two are drawn together, they understand each other, there is a harmonious feeling with both when in the presence of each other, and they become good friends and sometimes it is more; for this accounts for "love at first sight" of which we hear so much.

The blending of the magnetic auras is essential to best results in every phase of Spirit Mediumship including healing by laying on of hands.

In most cases the mind and will of the healer and the subject may cause the auras to blend, where there is no prejudice, suspicion, jealousies, or other unpleasant thing to disturb the harmony between them.

### DIAGNOSING THE CASE

The healer should take note of the nature of the disease, the physical condition of the patient, and the best way to apply the treatment should be considered. The patient should be placed in as comfortable a position as possible. The healer should know what disease he is attacking.

If the patient loves music, a little soft, gentle music is useful. The greater the harmony, the better the conditions will be and the better the mental and physical conditions are the greater will be the success.

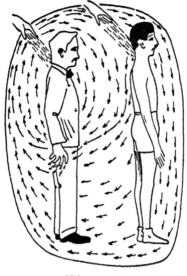

Figure 3

This figure 3 shows the spirit hand applying the spiritual forces to the base of the healer's brain while he is treating the patient. The spirit applies his wonderful healing forces to the nervous system of the healer, and the patient, when they are sufficiently mediumistic to receive it. When the spirit forces are applied to both healer and patient, the power is greatly multiplied. The spirit hand is charging the healer's nervous system with the spiritual forces as he manipulates the patient's entire body, throwing off the diseased magnetism by snapping it off his finger ends, preparatory to applying the healing forces to the patient's nervous system.

The spirit applies his forces to the base of the brain of the spiritual healer as shown above and charges his entire nervous system with its wonderful healing powers.

These treatments are usually more effective in private than in the public halls, because the minds of the healer and of the patient are more concentrated on the healing and they are not wondering what the audience thinks of this demonstration.

### PROOF OF ONE'S MEDIUMSHIP

The magnetism generated in the organism of the mortal is warm and forces generated by the spirit is without heat or is cold. The spirit applies his forces to the nerve center at the base of the brain of the healer and the patient as is shown in Figure 3, and the spirit forces being cold, coming in contact with the warm magnetism of the mortal, at this nerve center produces a chill, and this vibration passes down the spinal column and may reach throughout the entire body. Any person having this experience is a medium and may develop by making proper conditions if not already developed.

Figure 4

Figure 4 represents the healer's movements being made in circles which is in perfect accord with the moving principles of the universe; all of which moves in circles.

This figure also represents the spirit applying the spiritual forces to the base of the patient's brain. This is done when the patient is mediumistic and susceptible and absorbs them. When such is the case the healing power is greatly increased and the patient's return to health is more rapid.

We feel certain that many healers do not use patting, beating, and massaging as much as they should. I have had acute pain literally drummed out of me many times by beatings from the healer. I think healers should not in most cases cease treating until they have gone thoroughly over the body from head to foot, because this equalizes the circulation more completely. Mrs. Sprague often spent a half hour to an hour in treating a patient, which made her work very effectual. The harmonious blending of the spirit forces with the healer's magnetic aura and the patient's glad reception of it forms the necessary condition for good results in healing by laying on of hands.

The will of the spirit and of the healer controls these forces and makes use of them to accomplish the healing of a patient or in the production of other spirit manifestation.

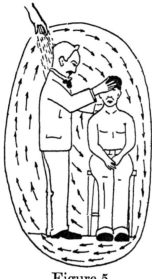

Figure 5

## HOW TO HEAL BY LAYING ON OF HANDS

Figure 5 represents the healer charging the patient's nervous system with the electro-magnetic, vital and spiritual forces.

Place the right hand, which is positive, on the patient's forehead, and the left hand, which is negative*, on the neck at the base of the brain. The right hand being positive throws

*If the healer is left handed, his left hand is positive and his right hand is negative and he should reverse their application.

out the vital magnetic force and the left being negative will receive it. This forms the circuit, the current passes through the brain of the patient, charging his entire nervous system with the healing forces in a short time. Most patients feel a tingle of the nerves throughout the entire body when being charged.

While doing this, the healer and patient should think how the forces operate; this places the patient in a receptive condition to receive the treatment. After the patient's system is thoroughly charged, the healer should go over his entire body from head to foot as represented in Figure No. 4 by making his movements in circles and snapping the diseased aura from his fingers, thus clearing the way for the healing forces. After this the healer may wash his hands, rub them together until they are hot, then apply them by slapping, patting, rubbing, and willing his healing forces to act upon these organs, placing his hands upon the diseased organs principally, thinking, and determinedly willing, a cure for his patient, *and as the last act of his treatment, he should make passes from the head of the pa-*

*tient to his feet, going all around him, gently*
*touching him or coming close to his body to*
*equalize and cause the gentle circulation of the*
*patient's magnetism.* Then the patient, if not
strong, should lie down quietly for a half
hour. A few minutes' sleep is *always* helpful
after receiving a treatment.

### HEALING BY LAYING ON OF HANDS
### DEVELOPS WITH PRACTICE

Cure for headache, sick headache, inflammation of the brain, etc. The healer should first
charge the brain and nervous system of the
patient as is shown in Figure 5. Then apply by
laying the hands upon the forehead and the
temples, rubbing gently, sending his magnetic
forces mentally to the work of removing the
congestion, and gently at first, passing the
hands down the spine and as the power increases and the patient will bear it, increase
the pressure upon the spine in a few manipula-
tions, after which manipulate the auras without rubbing the body a few times from the top
of his head to his feet along the back. If the
pain is not relieved at first, repeat this effort,
and if not helped, then probably the forces do

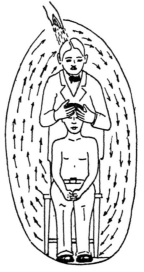

Figure 6

not blend well; but many can heal headaches at the first attempt. Many healers do not spend time enough in treating the patient for certain diseases.

## HEADACHES CAUSED FROM STOMACH TROUBLES

The stomach should be treated first after the nervous system has been charged, always rubbing downward unless the patient will belch gas freely. While doing so, let your strokes be upward while the patient throws out the gas, then rub downward steadily, slowly with mental determination to free the stomach. After this treat the head and spine as directed above.

In many cases of headache this detail is not necessary. All depends upon the healer's powers, the patient's receptivity, and the blending of their forces.

It is always well for any healer to know all he can about the human system and the correct way to treat. The more he knows the better work the spirit friends can do with him.

Figure 7 represents the healer placing the knee in the back of the patient, directly behind the lungs with his hands on the patient's shoulders, gently but firmly pressing the knee against the spine which gives the patient's lungs more room to expand when inhaling air.

The writer's life was saved after a bad fall, striking on his head and shoulders, by a healer treating him once in this manner.

Figure 7

One who has weak lungs may greatly improve them by practicing deep breathing, and this treatment of gentle pressure on the spine helps to expand the chest, allowing the lungs more room to develop. Many people do not breathe deeply enough and the lungs are not filled. Deep breathing is a healthful and profitable exercise. Lungs of a child may by deep breathing be grown, like cabbage in a good garden, and parents should see that their children develop good and efficient lung power by deep breathing.

Figure 8

Figure 8 shows another way to free the congested lungs, which is often used by Magnetic, Mental and Spiritual healers to free and expand the lungs.

Deep breathing is a wonderfully healthful exercise which is explained in another part of this work and Figures 7 and 8 present a very efficient and helpful method of developing lung power. The healer should take into consideration in every case, the physical condition of the patient, the state of his mind, the peculiarities of the disease, and know whether the disease is chronic or acute, and ask for, or desire spirit impressions regarding just how to treat it.

### ADAPTABILITY OF HEALER'S AND PATIENT'S FORCES

There must be a harmonious blending of the physical and mental forces of the healer and the patient for the best results. Mental forces and mental conditions affect the application and reception of the magnetic and spiritual auras, and the healer as well as the patient should keep his thoughts on the operation and the operators, while one is being treated.

### LAWS OF VIBRATION

Everything is in a state of vibration. Certain rates of vibration are necessary to produce certain results. The vibration of material things is comparatively slow when considered with the mental and spiritual vibrations.

Scientists have made a table of rates of vibrations and of the seven colors of the rainbow, they show that they number billions per second in some colors. Of course this is unthinkable, but spirits tell us that the vibrations of thought have an immensely higher rate than the vibration of the physical atoms, and the spiritual rate of vibration is almost infinitely more rapid than the mental vibrations of mortal man when measured by the standards of the mortal mind.

Some people may ask what has the law of vibration to do with healing by laying on of hands? In answer to this, I will say: it has very much indeed to do with healing. As an illustration, A patient has fever, the pulse running high. The vibratory action of the patient's entire system is in full harmony with this condition and its rate of action is governed by it. This is the natural law in action. Now, the Magnetic, Mental, and Spiritual healer appears and with words of kindness and promise assures the patient that he will be better soon. The healer places his hands in cold water, rubs them together a little, then places his right hand on the patient's forehead and his left hand at the Sensorium or base of the brain, charging the nervous system with his healing forces. The quieting, calming influences of the healer's magnetic and vital forces quiets the rapid heart-beats and spreads calmness throughout the patient's entire system. Then the healer gently strokes the patient's body, making long strokes from the head to the feet, snapping the patient's diseased aura from his finger ends, as illustrated by Figure No. 3 on page 64 and going all around the patient as he lies on the bed, if he is not able to sit up. Lastly the healer, after bathing his hands again, should equalize and cause the gentle and calm circulation of the patient's magnetism and putting him to sleep if possible.

The patient should then spend a little time in sleeping. The author has seen Mrs. Sprague free a patient of fever in this manner in a few minutes, hundreds of times. The efficiency of the treatment by laying on of hands is certainly proven by the Spiritual healers who follow the above-mentioned method. This treatment changes the rapid rate of vibration to the normal rate and the patient is relieved of the fever. For more on the subject of vibration see pages 98-99.

### EASY DEVELOPMENT OF MAGNETIC AND SPIRITUAL HEALING

#### AUTHOR'S BROTHER A HEALING MEDIUM

*Perfectly Healed by One Treatment, the First Treatment This Healer Ever Gave*

A person may be a magnetic healer and get little or no help from the spirit side of life, though such cases are rare with those who follow healing the sick by laying on of hands, because spiritual development is brought about through the practice of magnetic healing. The author's brother, Franklin, developed clairvoyance, clairaudience, and inspirational speaking without sitting for development at all. A medium told him he had great healing powers and shortly after that, one of his neighbors became very ill of inflammatory rheumatism; another neighbor who was present when the spirits told brother of his wonderful power, sent for him and went with him to treat this patient. My brother was not a Spiritualist and did not know how to proceed. The patient was suffering terribly; his cries were heard in a neighbor's house across the street. The poor, sick man they said had not slept for three nights and one could not touch the bedding when he asked them to move his hand a little, but he would cry out with pain.

Mr. Clark, who went with my brother, told him to pass his hand up and down above the bed covering as the man lay facing the front of the bed. This he did. The man ceased to cry out. Mr. Clark told Franklin then to lay back the clothes and rub the patient's back, which he did. The pain had stopped, and in a few minutes the man went to sleep and in three days the patient went out of the house and had no more rheumatism.

My brother then began treating people and he was called for miles around and his development came rapidly. He began to see and locate disease, tell its cause, etc. I have never known a better healer or a better Medical

Clairvoyant in all my long experience than my dear brother, Franklin Sprague, and he developed his wonderful powers by treating people by laying on of hands, and not by sitting in developing circles at all. His healing gifts were magnetic and spiritual. He was often controlled by spirits.

I have told this true story in the hope that it may give encouragement to healers whose development may be slow, as some mediums are not developed as rapidly as others.

I knew a barber who said he developed his healing powers by being in the different magnetisms of his customers in the barber's chair. He never sat for development. Magnetic and Spiritual healing is one of the easiest phases of mediumship to develop when one is mediumistic and magnetic.

I have known perfect cures of cases of long years' standing to be accomplished in one treatment. It is a fact that I was cured by my brother Franklin, of periodical sick headaches, in which I had suffered untold agonies at regular intervals for twenty years, and he cured me in five minutes, and I have never had a single touch of it since, and fifty years have passed since he cured me.

Read the facts of this wonderful case in the next article.

### THE AUTHOR PERMANENTLY CURED BY ONE TREATMENT BY THE LAYING ON OF HANDS

The author of this book has been cured of disease at different times during his life work in the field of Spiritualism and once before he became a Spiritualist. The record of this case appeared in my book entitled "A Future Life Demonstrated," which at this time is out of print. Therefore I think best to republish these facts in this book. They are as follows:

My brother Franklin was a wonderful medium. He was a clairvoyant, clairaudient, trance and inspirational speaker, and a fine test medium. He excelled as a medical clairvoyant and Magnetic and Spiritual healer, curing many patients after the regular doctors had failed.

### CURED BY SPIRIT POWER

From childhood until thirty-two years of age I was the victim of periodical "sick headaches," they came on me once or twice a month regularly. One night in the year 1879, at our home in North Boston, New York, I was awakened from sleep by one of those raging headaches. I could not remain in bed. Mrs. Sprague did not then know of her wonderful mediumship, or perhaps she could have cured me. However, she was a good nurse, and tried every remedy she could think of to relieve my distress, but her efforts were of no avail. My poor head persisted in aching. The pain had no compassion on my nerves, but continued relentlessly until I felt I could endure it no longer. The reader who has been the victim of such terrible brain spasms will understand what I was suffering, without further explanation.

While I was walking backward and forward across the room I cried out in my agony. I felt I could not endure the pain another minute, when Mrs. Sprague proposed going over to my sister's where my brother Franklin was stopping for the night, and get him to come and treat me. "Oh," said I, "Franklin can do me no good!" How foolish an unbeliever may be! But we could think of nothing else to do as there was no doctor nearer than four miles away, so she went after brother and he came. I was sitting in a chair holding my head with both hands when he entered the door. He greeted me with a kindly "good morning," and asked what was the matter with me. I explained that I had the worst headache that anyone could have and live. He smiled pleasantly and said he would cure me in five minutes. "If you do I will give you fifty dollars" I said quickly. "I would not take your money under any circumstances," said he, "but I will demand that you acknowledge the fact that I cured you." "Franklin," said I, "if you will cure me or make me believe that I have no pain, I will publish it to the world." And here let me say that after twenty-eight years' delay I fulfilled that promise. It is a poor paymaster who withholds the payment of a debt like that so long, but I am glad to be able to fulfill that promise again at this late day. The above was published after I had been cured and enjoyed freedom from those headaches and now I am republishing these blessed truths after fifty years of freedom from those terrible brain spasms. Oh, how wonderful and blessed is Magnetic and Spiritual healing!

After I developed as a medium the spirit friends gave us lessons on mediumship of different phases including Magnetic, Mental and Spiritual healing and they explained my case of sick headache and how the cure was accomplished, as follows: The brain is composed of nerve cells so small they cannot be seen with the natural eye. In health those nerve cells are filled with nerve fluid, but they become empty and collapse, and this unnatural condition creates inflammation and causes intense nerve pain. My brother being full of the electromagnetic and vitalizing forces and directing them to my brain by his own will, simply by holding his right hand, which is positive, upon my forehead and his left hand, which is negative, at the back of my head, at the base of the brain, the current of his healing aura going out of his positive right hand passing through my brain, and entering his negative left hand going on through his body formed the circuit and charged my brain with these nerve forces and those delicate little nerve cells were stimulated into action, opened up and received the nerve fluid that placed them in normal condition, and my cure was completed, and I have never had the sick headache since that day, which is now fifty-one years ago.

The operation of the Magnetic and Spiritual healing forces are so simple, natural, and so powerful, and so easily developed that no family should be without its own healing medium.

### A TEST OF MIND AND WILL-POWER

It was reported that a man was placed in a horizontal position upon balance scales and they were evenly balanced. He was then told to think his blood to his feet. He did so and his feet went down. Then he was instructed to think his blood to his head. He did so and his head went down. The statement said the experiment was repeated and in each case it was proved that his mind sent the blood back and forth which caused the scales to respond to his will showing that the mind has power

over the circulation of the blood. It is proven
in many ways that the mind acts upon the different organs of the body. We know that this
is true, therefore we should learn how to think
for good health and then practice it.

### A THOUGHT FOR THE UNBELIEVER

It is true that some people who do not understand healing by laying on of hands may
scoff at the claims made for its efficiency and
perhaps doubt the facts presented in this work.
To such skeptic we would say, If a pocket
handkerchief or any piece of cloth was carried
into the presence of a smallpox patient, a yel-
low fever patient, or any patient suffering
with a contagious disease, and the article cir-
culated around him in his aura never touching
his body, then placed in an envelope, sealed
and sent to you, Mr. Skeptic, you could hardly
be induced to open the envelope if written on
it were the facts telling what it contained.

This shows that you believe more in the
power of magnetism than you really think you
do.

Man is a psychic and magnetic and psychic or spiritual healing is the most natural and potent method. Jesus, his apostles and disciples, practiced it successfully but the Christian church, not understanding it, and teaching that it was a miracle, and not being able to perform miracles, let it drop and now Spiritualism is teaching them that it is natural phenomena.

## MAN IS A SPIRIT AND SHOULD CONTROL HIS BODY

Man should control his body because he is intelligent and can know what is best for it. If the spirit does not control the body, the body may control the spirit. The body is not intelligent and may lead to excesses, if not controlled by the intelligent spirit.

## "MAN, KNOW THYSELF"

This is a great command and should be accompanied with instructions how to know himself. There is but one proper way to study oneself and that is to look for the motive that inspires every desire and trace it to its source if possible; and there learn if it was born of the spirit or of the flesh, and if it is legitimate and proper, or illegitimate and improper. After the spirit has decided the question, if it is improper, it should put the desire away by using the power of will, courting a complacent spirit and making the very best of the situation; looking upon the bright side of the subject, knowing that when we are right we cannot go wrong. Every thought, every impulse and every emotion should be handled in the same way. If an evil thought projects itself upon the consciousness, by the use of the will, it should be put away and beautiful and good thoughts should take its place. Mental healing is as wonderful as physical healing, and they work together beautifully and naturally.

### THOUGHTS ARE REAL TANGIBLE THINGS

Thoughts are things we think and what we think we have named thoughts, therefore thought is something. Thought is powerful and leads the thinker to act. Thought builds houses, automobiles, airplanes, everything, and builds them in the minds of men before the mechanic strikes a blow. Therefore thought is something. A good thought is a good thing and an evil thought is a bad thing.

It cannot be successfully denied that thought has great power to heal the sick or to destroy good health. Deep thought laid the Atlantic cable, discovered the X-Ray, worked out the radio, and will finally accomplish the world's peace. Thought is a most powerful thing and when properly applied with healing by laying on of hands, proves its great efficiency.

### THOUGHT AS A HEALTH PRESERVER

Many New Thought societies and teachers, in giving their health lessons, make the great mistake of ignoring the law of cause and effect, when the truth is that every effect is the result of a natural cause. Whether it be Magnetic, Mental, or Spiritual healing; whether it be "Faith cure," "Prayer cure," "Divine healing," "Emmanuelism," or any other specially named method of cure employed.

Nature's laws govern every successful method of healing, just as they govern all other phenomena that occur. There is no secret method underlying any genuine manifestation of healing which is known only to certain "masters," "adepts," "Commissioned Christian Science healers," Magnetic and Spiritual healers," or any other class of people. No persons have received such secret healing powers through any "Special Providence," "Divine call," or in any other "miraculous manner." All that is known of the operations of "Spiritual," "occult" and other methods of healing and all that the spirit friends have given regarding healing and "Spiritual Philosophy" are open and free to all people of the world and have no particle or coloring of miracle attached to them. Therefore, we may beware of all who lay claim to secret, special, unknown, or miraculous powers.

Every act of our lives, every thought we think, every impulse that possesses us has its influence upon our health and our enjoyment of life and what we most need to know is how to control our thoughts, our impulses and our actions. There is no legitimate reason why we may not control them when we have learned how to do so; and one of the purposes of this book is to teach how to control ourselves and keep within the realm of the harmonious vibrations of health and happiness.

Dr. Andrew Jackson Davis, that great and good man, and father of Modern Spiritualism, has given us many grand truths and splendid precepts, principles and aphorisms, one of which I will mention here, for it is one that we may always apply with great advantage in the development of our higher powers. Here it is: "Behold! Here is thy magic staff. Under all circumstances keep an even mind. Take it, Try it, Walk with it, Talk with it. Lean on it. Believe on it. Forever!"

The person who fulfills this precept, keeping an even mind under all circumstances will never become angry, sad, discouraged, revengeful, jealous, or hateful, and will of a necessity be always happy, while traveling the broad highway to physical health and spiritual unfoldment.

We should learn to become positive to in-harmony and negative to harmony, sealing ourselves against the former and becoming receptive to the latter.

Universal spirit, universal intelligence, universal energy, universal good, and universal love, permeates every part of the universe. We are a part of this magnificent universe and are endowed with a portion of all of the above-named attributes and qualities belonging to it. We have power to will our own physical forces into activity, increase their flow and thus eliminate disease from our systems. We can equalize our own vital forces and think them into harmonious vibration, and under this condition health must follow as a natural consequence. Magnetic, Mental and Spiritual healers are great helps in this development. We must first develop these powers before we can use them.

### MAN A SPIRIT

We are spirits now and we possess bodies. To illustrate, my body is not I. It is mine. It is an instrument of many parts, a series of machines run by the power of a great dynamo. Through this dynamo I generate the power, and I, being the spirit operator, apply it to each little delicate organ and keep them all running. My thoughts affect the rate of my heart-beats. Excessive joy may quicken the rate of my heart's action. Great fear and fright may stop its beating.

If we can affect the rate of the beating of our heart by the use of our thought, may we not increase the action of the other organs of our bodies by the use of the same power? We certainly can do so, when we have assumed the intelligent mastery over our own domain. Then let us say to the solar plexus, generate more vital forces, and disseminate the needed energy throughout the entire system. Let us speak to the liver and tell it to perform its allotted functions thoroughly and well. Let us tell the blood to cleanse itself from all impurities as it traverses the winding ways of the arterial and veinous system as the brooks and rivers purify themselves on their way from the mountains to the sea. Running water purifies itself, why should not the beautiful crimson stream that flows through our veins and arteries purify itself in the same way, if we give it sufficient air by deep breathing and sufficient freedom through the proper exercise of the body and the determination of the mind? Say to your digestive organs, I shall supply you with only such food as your capacity is qualified to care for and assimilate properly, and you *must* take care of it. You *will* properly digest it. You *shall* do it.

Whenever you have given these orders to the different organs of the body you *must not think you have done your full part of the work,* but you must keep in mind the fact that the responsibility all still lies with you, and you must continually hold the thought and determine the fact that each organ is doing exactly what you ordered it to do. "If at first you don't succeed, try, try again" becoming more determined to succeed. Good news has cured bed-ridden patients. Fear has caused instant death. If thought has such control over our lives it is plain to be seen that proper thinking will generate harmony and harmony produces good health.

This physical body is my Empire, my spirit is the ruler of this empire. I will rule it with firmness, with justice, with kindness, with love. All within my little domain shall be harmonious; no part of it shall have cause to complain of neglect or improper treatment by its ruler. Every portion of this empire shall have equal opportunity for development, for expression, and for the fulfillment of its duties and its mission. I shall ever remain solicitous and manifest a tender care over all of my beloved possessions.

Science teaches that matter cannot be destroyed, that there is no dead matter and our Spiritual Philosophy says that spirit and matter are inseparable whether in this world or in the spirit world; that life is an active principle of matter.*

It is beautiful to cultivate the powers of the physical body; but to unfold the physical, the mental and the spiritual faculties and powers,

*Matter of the spiritual world is said to be rarified, refined, sublimated, etherialized, spiritualized, matter or substance.

bringing them into harmony and unity, is still better and should be the development sought.

## TO THE WORKERS FOR SPIRITUALISM

You are students in school
Working by nature's rule
There is nothing in life you need fear.
When you each do your best,
Spirit friends do the rest
In fulfilling your mission while here.

In sickness and distress
Great sufferers you bless
Healing the sick in body and mind.
I can truthfully state
You work early and late,
Through you comfort and health many find.

You are faithful and true
In the work that you do
In time to come will bless everyone,
Who are led to perceive,
Sufferings you relieve,
In work you are doing and have done.

The vital forces generated in the physical form of the spiritual healer are used by spirits to heal the sick.

The spirit healer controls these forces through the manipulation of the mind of the medium through whom he operates.

In the process of thinking we draw the vital forces, which are generated in the system, to the brain where we utilize them in thinking. The activity of the mind throws them off like the exhaust of a steam engine is thrown off.

One who is sufficiently clairvoyant may sometimes see the light thought waves as they flash from the brain of one who is actively thinking. A person under spirit control or strong spirit influence uses more of this vital force than when thinking in a normal way.

Under this active inspiration, the medium's head becomes cold because of the mingling of the spirit forces — which are cold — with the nerve auras and vital forces of the medium; though the medium's forces are generated in a warm body and are warm.

The desire to heal another is strengthened

by the will to do it. Mothers heal the child with a kiss. These forces are applied affectionately and the suggestion completes the work.

The nervous organism acts similar to a wireless telegraphic plant sending out these vital healing forces through the psychic ether and it acts upon that ether through the law of vibration similar to the action of Marconi's electric waves upon the atmosphere. The spirit directing these forces applies them to the patient though he be at a distance from the human battery—the medium—in whom they are generated.

### ABSENT TREATMENTS

Distance is as nothing to the transmission of thought. It is as easy to reach a person with a thought suggestion when many miles away as when a thousand feet away from the operator, if the brain of the receiver is in tune with its rate of vibration.

A thought travels on and on until it becomes absorbed in other psychic vibrations of the occult or spiritual ethers. Some people are much more receptive to thought vibrations and suggestions than are others, very mediumistic people sometimes being able to receive them almost to perfection. This is proven in experimental telepathy. If the suggestion reaches the patient that the operator is to treat at a certain time, and the patient consents willingly, and better still if he is anxious for the treatment, this condition of mind connects him with the operator and aids in the patient's receptivity of the operator's health suggestions.

*Physical changes are produced through mental efforts.* We may make our hearts beat faster or slower by mental effort. We can think or will its more rapid movements and thus quicken the circulation of our blood, or we can calm the heart-beats caused by excitement by using the will and making such suggestion. Mental suggestion is a most potent power for good, and Spiritualism is giving the world its first or primary lessons upon the subject. This power may be developed by practice.

In treating an absent patient mentally the active forces are greatly strengthened by the co-operation of the patient with the operator, and the patient having knowledge of the fact that he is being treated greatly strengthens the forces; therefore, it is better for the patient to know the time and purpose of the operator and still better for him to enter into co-operation mentally with the operator. Spirits then can co-operate better with them both. A person may, if mediumistic, receive help physically and mentally from the operator and the spirit friends, and never know from whence his relief comes, or without his co-operation. In such cases, as in the other one mentioned, the operator becomes the battery from which the spirit operators draw the forces needed in repairing the physical body. These they unite with the spiritual forces which they generate and apply to the patient. Patients are healed in this manner without knowing the source from which health comes and sometimes, even, without the knowledge of the operator.

It is much better, however, to have the hearty co-operation of all three, the operator, the patient and the spirits. Possibly as much at times depends upon the patient's attitude of mind and his receptivity to the healing forces as upon the healer's power, though all are needed to produce the best results.

Through co-operation many people are cured of diseases, bad habits and vices by the methods explained above.

The surroundings of patients have much to do with their recovery from illness. Everyone around them should maintain a happy, confident, state of mind, never referring to the possibility of their not recovering good health.

They should not talk of the patient's disease only to impress the patient with the idea of his or her recovery.

### MRS. SPRAGUE A SPLENDID HEALER AND MEDIUM FOR OTHER PHASES

We traveled together for thirteen years as missionaries of the National Spiritualist Association, working in thirty different states of the Union, both of us preaching, teaching and demonstrating the truths of Spiritualism by following our lectures with spirit messages, and tests, and also in private work. Mrs. Sprague in addition to this, healed the sick by laying on of hands, from the Atlantic to the Pacific coasts.

We were aided in our studies of mediumship by our spirit helpers. They taught us many facts regarding Magnetic, Mental and Spiritual healing and aided us in our experiments, while teaching our psychic classes.

Mrs. Sprague was a Spiritualist speaker, an ordained minister, and platform test medium, and hundreds and thousands of American citizens can testify to her success in that particular sphere of spiritual work. She gave private readings; held circles and seances, besides aiding in the development of mediums in our psychic classes and elsewhere. She was clairvoyant, clairaudient and clairsentient. She was a personating medium and an impressional medium and healed the sick by laying on of hands and practiced her blessed gifts for the good of humanity for nearly forty-eight years.

### HEALING WITHOUT PERSONAL CONTACT AND BY USING MAGNETIZED ARTICLES

Many spiritual healers are able to heal without coming in personal contact with the patient. Distance is not a hindrance to spiritual healing. Spirits convey the forces they generate, mingled with the healer's aura, to the patient who may not be near the earthly healer. When the healer and patient have an understanding regarding the matter, each knowing the exact time for their sitting and both putting their minds upon it, the healer wills to send his healing powers, the patient becomes passive and attentive to the reception of the magnetic and spiritual forces; then the spirits have the necessary conditions to accomplish the work.

Matt. VIII, 13. Jesus healed at a distance this child through the same laws as the Spiritual healers do today. This was no miracle.

### THE PATIENT'S MIND, IF RIGHT, HELPS THE HEALER

Mind controls the body and its movements. If one's mind is right it becomes a great and mighty power in regaining and preserving one's physical health.

Thinking good and happy thoughts to become inspired with that class of thoughts, causes one to live the happy life. Peace, love, joy, laughter, kindness, and all such good things embodied in one's daily life generates harmony and harmony produces good health, and good health produces harmony. Inharmony produces ill health and ill health produces inharmony. One should choose harmony, live a harmonious life if one would be healthy and enjoy life.

Mrs. Sprague healed people at a distance that she had never seen. I will mention one case. A lady in Illinois wrote her and asked if she could diagnose diseases and heal at a distance. She took the letter in her left hand, asked the spirits if they could show her what was the woman's trouble. She immediately suffered nerve pains in the back of the neck and left shoulder and was unable to lift her hand to her head. She had hard work to throw off this condition, but in a few minutes she was relieved. She wrote and told the lady her condition, the cause of it, and sent her some magnetized paper and the lady replied to the letter saying: "Mrs. Sprague, you must be a wonderful sensitive for you got my condition perfectly." Mrs. Sprague's magnetized paper charged with the spirit forces healed many. She was controlled to manipulate and magnitize the blotting paper she sent to the lady and the lady was relieved at once by applying it. Mrs. Sprague healed other people by magnetizing paper and sending it to some whom she never saw and to acquaintances who received benefit therefrom.

St. Paul, of the Christian Bible, was a spirit medium for many phases, the same as our mediums are, and he was a good magnetic and spiritual healer, with powers very similar to those of Mrs. Sprague, and he healed at a distance with magnetized articles just as she did; the Bible says so. Acts XIX, 11 says: "And God wrought special miracles by the hands of Paul."

12th verse: "So that from his body are brought unto the sick, handkerchiefs or aprons, and the diseases departed from them and the evil spirits went out of them." They believed evil spirits caused disease.

Neither Mrs. Sprague nor the writer believe that evil spirits cause disease, but the writers of the Scriptures must have believed it, because it says Jesus cast them out and the sick were healed.

Matt. VIII, 16 says: "When even was come, they brought unto Him (Jesus) many that were possessed with devils; and he cast out the spirits with his word and healed all that were sick." These prophets of God believed that evil spirits caused disease. Few people believe that to-day.

Luke VIII, 2: "And certain women which had been healed of evil spirits and infirmities, Mary Magdalene out of whom went seven devils." Were they counted as they came out? Did they see them? I cannot believe it. I never saw a devil.

Luke VII, 21: Jesus said to have "cured many of their infirmities and plagues and of evil spirits."

Mark IX, 17-29: Epilepsy thought to be evil spirits. Jesus casts this supposed evil spirit out and heals the patient of epilepsy, sometimes called falling fits.

JESUS, A PERSONATING MEDIUM

Matt. VIII, 17: Jesus takes on conditions

of patients as Mrs. Sprague did. She was a personating medium, too. This 17th verse says, "That it might be fulfilled which was spoken by Esaias the prophet, saying: Himself took our infirmities and bare our sicknesses."

John IV, 46-54: Jesus healed the nobleman's son without seeing him or being near him, because the nobleman had faith in Jesus and believed he could do it.

### GIVING ABSENT TREATMENT

The healer should sit down by himself, where all is quiet. It is well to think a silent prayer to his spirit helpers. This helps to place him in the proper condition to receive their assistance and attracts them near him.

His only thought should be of sympathy for his patient and a determination to heal him.

Though the patient be a great distance away, it matters little with some healers, for distance is nothing to the spirit. The healer should picture in his mind his patient as sitting right before him and think the laying on of hands and the movements he would make if the patient was with him.

After many years of wide experience we can truly say we have found no healing power that is so easily developed, so pleasantly applied, and so quickly effectual, as Magnetic, Mental and Spiritual healing. We have been greatly blessed by its use in raising our family and gladly testify to its value.

MENTAL AND SPIRITUAL HEALING PERMANENT

*Major Mathews Cured of Tobacco Habit Instantly. This Was Not a Miracle, but Great as Bible Miracles*

Mrs. Major C. H. Mathews of New Philadelphia, Ohio, related the following experience: Dr. Schwartz, a magnetic healer and medium, held a circle at Ashley, Ohio, camp meeting, and before taking their seats in the circle, Dr. Schwartz asked the members if any of them were possessed of bad habits and said that he would cure them if they wished to get rid of them. Major Mathews asked to be cured of the tobacco habit and from that evening forward he never used tobacco in any form, *never had any desire for it* though he had been an inveterate smoker for fifty years. He tried to see if he could use it, but could not.

### CURED BY ABSENT TREATMENTS

Mrs. Mathews, long before Mr. Mathews was cured, wrote Dr. Schwartz, sending him $1.00 for absent treatments for her arm with which she had been troubled for many years. Sometimes she could not get it up to comb her hair and sometimes she could not get it down after having had it up for a time. The trouble was in the shoulder.

Dr. Schwartz, though then in Boston, Mass. and Mrs. Mathews in New Philadelphia, Ohio, cured her entirely. Mrs. Mathews was instructed to sit at a certain hour each day. And now, after twenty-five or more years, she says she has never been troubled with it in the least. She was permanently cured. If these two cases had occurred in Christ's time they would have been given to the world as miracles.

There are thousands of cases of patients being cured by spiritual healers in a similar manner and of various kinds of diseases in this country today as is well known to those who are interested but are seldom mentioned in the public newspapers, though some magazines are quite free to publish them.

Major Mathews in conversations with the writer, fully corroborated the above statements.

### SPIRITUAL TRUTHS REVEALED TO CHRISTIANS BY SPIRITUALISTS

The Christian Church of the world should not feel offended because the Spiritualists have discovered one of their mistakes. They have thought and still insist that the phenomena on which Christianity is based (much of which is identical with the phenomena of Spiritualism of today) was miraculous. Spiritualists have proven that they are natural phenomena, and furthermore have learned, and are teaching the world the natural and scientific method of their production.

It would appear better in the minds of just people if the Christians would express their gratitude, and give thanks to the Spiritualists, showing their appreciation of the discovery of this great mistake of theirs, and rejoice at being set aright. Many good Christians are doing this, but the Christian church itself is either denying the truth of this discovery and revelation of Spiritualism, or grudgingly acknowledging its truths in part, as is being preached by the liberal Christians but they seldom give the credit to Spiritualism for the discovery of the facts. While the more orthodox, the Fundamentalists, go on condemning Spiritualism as the works of the devil. Just as the Jews accused Jesus of having a devil, and as Jesus said they accused John the Baptist of having a devil (Matt. XI, 18).

John VIII, 52: "Then said the Jews unto him, (unto Jesus), Now we know that Thou hast a devil." This became the habit of the unbelievers in Jesus, as it is now with the Adventists.

Adventists should be careful or they may place themselves with the Jewish accusers of Jesus, and also place the Spiritualists in the position of Jesus. Adventists have had the habit of condemning Spiritualism as being of the devil for the last seventy years. I have eighteen bound books, and pamphlets, in my library written by Christians; mostly by Adventists, condemning Spiritualism, and misrepresenting it by declaring it is all of the devil.

For all of the 82 years of modern Spiritualism, some of the orthodox Christian churches have condemned it as being of the devil, and many of its ministers and some M. D.'s of this land of the free and good homes of many religions have condemned and religiously opposed its methods of healing by laying on of hands, as was done to Jesus of Nazareth by the church and civil authorities of his day, according to Scripture. And these, our opponents of Spiritualism, went before many legislatures at different times introducing bills that made it a crime to practice healing by laying on of hands in this so-called Christian country, and too for healing the sick. Many of *our Spiritual healers have suffered much for doing what Jesus said his followers should do.* "He that believeth on me, the works that I do shall he do also, and greater work than these shall he do because I go unto my Father." (John XIV, 12.) These are the words of Jesus, according to Scripture. Then who are the followers of Jesus according to this statement of His? Why, this proves that the Spiritualists are the true believers in Jesus and it also shows that the opponents of Spiritualism are the unbelievers in Jesus.

There are many, many Scripture passages to prove that Spiritualists are doing what Jesus said believers in him would do.

Healers by laying on of hands were fined and some doubtless were imprisoned under the laws made by medical men. Bills were presented in different state legislatures that healing by laying on of hands be considered practicing medicine and provisions made for fine and imprisonment for such unlicensed offenders. But since Spiritualists have proven to many Christians that healing by laying on of hands is not a miracle as taught by Christianity, but is a natural and scientific fact, as well as a powerful method of healing the sick, many Christian churches all over the land are taking it up in the hope of saving it to the church. May success attend them, mankind needs healing.

The following article is just one little

example of the way our mediums used to be harrassed and persecuted in this Christian country. This was published in the Progressive Thinker of Chicago, Ill.

### "ANOTHER OUTRAGE"

"To the Editor:—In the town of Bisbee, Arizona, Mrs. Jennie Darrell, an ordained Spiritual minister, was arrested and fined to the amount of $50, for holding a spiritual meeting in the only available hall in the place.

"The cause for complaint was based on the fact that she charged an admission at the door. Inasmuch as religious rights are not respected by the officials of Bisbee, Mrs. Darrell was compelled to pay her fine or go to the county jail.

"She had just paid her fine when another warrant was issued against her for being a clairvoyant. Terrible laws exist in Arizona against clairvoyance and mediums.

"Being timely warned by a friend that there were papers out against her, and wanting no more of Bisbee injustice, Mrs. Darrell started, at night, for Tombstone, the county seat, a distance of 35 miles, walking the whole distance in the dead of night, and arriving there footsore and weary, she took the train for Tuscan, thereby avoiding the officers. Arizona is a land of deserts, and to describe her night trip over these arid wastes would be heartrending. The officer who arrested Mrs. Darrell is a man of very bad reputation. Under the cloak of his office he throttles the truth and persecutes a lone woman who is trying to elevate mankind. Such is law and justice in Arizona.

"Mrs. Darrell is on her way to San Bernardino, Cal., where she hopes to regain her religious rights to worship God as she deems fit. CORRESPONDENT."

Tuscan, Ariz.

There are worse things of recent occurrence, showing the great injustice and persecution of Spiritualists and their mediums of which I shall write a book later.

SPIRITS HEAL A CHRISTIAN THROUGH HER OWN MEDIUMSHIP—A TRUE STORY OF SPIRITS HEALING A CHRISTIAN WITH BUT ONE TREATMENT

The story of the cure was current in the vicinity of our home among Christians and the writer visited the patient and heard the story from the patient's own lips. She and her husband were strong church members whom I had known for many years and their word was perfectly good.

I will not give her name here, but will call her Mrs. G. B. The following is her story: She said the doctors had given up her case. She was bed ridden for four years with milk leg. The church members and minister surrounded her bed and prayed for her recovery at different times and she had prayed daily for relief from the first of her affliction and one night she said she began praying in her bed when alone at eight o'clock and she prayed until twelve o'clock, four hours continuously. "I never prayed so earnestly in my life," said she. "I put my soul into the prayer, asking Jesus to come and heal me and as the clock was striking the hour of twelve, my bed began to shake. It shook so hard that it fairly rattled. Oh, then Mr. Sprague, I knew Jesus had come to heal me. Following this my flesh began to tingle and it felt prickly all over me. Then I began to shake and my flesh seemed to shake loose on my bones. This experience lasted for some minutes, then all was quiet and Jesus said to me, 'You are now well, arise, arise,' and I arose, kneeled down by my bedside and thanked God and Christ for my deliverance. I got back into bed and slept until morning. When I awoke and arose I kneeled and thanked God and the Master again for my deliverance and dressed myself and walked to the kitchen, and from that day to this I have never been sick at all, but have been able to work and I have had three years of good health. My heart overflows with thankfulness to my Creator and to my beloved Master for this miracle in my favor."

She was a good soul, a good Christian woman, and this was a blessed demonstration of spirit power and proves to Spiritualists who are acquainted with similar cases, First: That this dear invalid was a medium or she could not have reached the condition alone necessary to receive the spirit's healing power.

Second: She passed through experiences that Spiritualists are perfectly familiar with, such as the bed shaking, her flesh prickling, and shaking, etc. Third: She was healed as thousands of good Spiritualists over the world have been and are being healed. Spirit phenomena sometimes occur among Christians in these later days, even though ridiculed and condemned by a certain class of uninformed Christians.

### THE HEALER'S JOYFUL MESSAGE

I do employ my time with joy,
  In relieving mortal pain,
Making them well, I'm glad to tell
  Much pleasure is my gain.

When sickness comes to anyone
  And I am led to know it,
I do my best and I am blest,
  Helping them to outgrow it.

I am well paid, the angels aid
  Me in the work I'm doing,
My patients sad, but are made glad,
  While I'm my work pursuing.

Welcome each one that to me come,
  The sorrowful and grieving,
And I am glad, they're no more sad,
  When they from me are leaving.

My mission's good; that's understood.
    And I rejoice to fill it.
The spirits true help me to do,
    It's blessed thus to view it.

And while I live my strength I'll give
    As freely as 'tis given;
It is my joy, time I'll employ,
    Till I am called to heaven.

So come who will, I'm working still,
    To relieve each one from pain,
It's well with me, as all may see,
    Doing good is my great gain.

### WISE SPIRIT GUIDES NOT ARBITRARY

Wise spirits never become arbitrary, dictatory, domineering controls. They give advice and in various ways lend assistance to their mediums in their efforts to learn and instruct others. Like attracts like, and a medium when developed may be controlled by a certain spirit or he may refuse to be. No spirit can control a medium without his consent or against his will.

The following statements of Dr. LaMotte Sage embody a number of valuable facts which every hypnotist and his subject, every healer and his patient, and every other spirit medium and every Spiritualist and all spirit controls should understand.

### DR. LAMOTTE SAGE'S VIEWS OF HYPNOTISM

1. "No one can be hypnotized against his will."

2. "No one can be hypnotized unless he complies with certain conditions and does his part to bring about that state."

3. "Anyone who is hypnotized may have done more himself to induce the state than the operator has done."

4. "The hypnotist possesses no special power nor can he gain permanent control over anyone or absolute control even temporarily, without the subject's consent."

5. "To be hypnotized in no respect shows a weakness, nor is the condition in any sense a pathological one."

6. "Hypnotism of itself is absolutely free from harm."

This expresses our views of this subject and we have been hypnotized by mortal hypnotists, and by spirit hypnotists thousands of times, and the process is the same. Their methods the same, and the effects on the medium or subject are the same. To be hypnotized one must place himself in the same condition he would to go to sleep.

### HYPNOTISM

Idiots cannot be hypnotized. Weak-minded persons never make good hypnotic subjects. People possessing large ideality make the best subjects. Those who are sensitive in organization and are endowed with vivid imaginations, possessing large ideality, easily subjected to mental impressions, mentally alert, and quick to discern are the best subjects for the hypnotists and for the spirit operator.

Positive persons are not so easily hypnotized, but they make the best subjects for spirit operators, as well as for the hypnotist on the mortal side of life, when once they are placed under control. Such subjects or mediums constitute a class by themselves and through the development of their natural powers, are able to become very positive or very negative as occasion may require. Positive to undesirable influences and negative to desirable ones. Our beloved spirit helper and guide, E. V. Wilson, was a King in this class. This is the development that every medium should strive to attain, as it is absolutely safe to use in any place. Such mediums have no fear of undeveloped spirits.

"It is claimed on good authority that hypnosis is only natural sleep artificially produced and brought to a higher state." (Prof. M. McCaslin, Ph.D.)

A medium may be controlled by a spirit operator and a hypnotic subject may be hypnotized by a hypnotist in the mortal form, either subject of the transaction may become unconscious under the control, or they may remain in a conscious state though controlled to do the wish of their operators.

The spirit hypnotist or control manifests a much greater power over his medium than is possible for the hypnotist in the physical form to use upon his subject, yet it may be possible, in time to come, that men in the mortal may develop powers that will greatly transcend those manifested by the spirits at the present time; but when mortals have reached that state of development, the spirits will have acquired still greater powers over their mediums and will remain a long way in the lead. This world will have progressed greatly, and Spiritualism will have become firmly grounded as are other sciences, because Evolution is the prevailing law of both states of existence.

### HYPNOTISM AS A HEALING FORCE

Hypnotism stimulates the faculties of mind and sometimes appears to create new powers; though this is not always the case; but the mental faculties or qualities of mind that may not have been discerned before are brought to the front.

Hypnotism is included in the laws governing mediumship. Through its laws the functions of any faculty may be suspended for a time and its action restored, not only uninjured, but greatly improved and strengthened in its power to perform its natural functions.

Through hypnotism, the same as by the practice of mediumship, many diseases may be permanently cured when proper conditions are made for it; though spirit mediumship is much more potent on account of the fact that the spirit control operating through a medium is in possession of a better knowledge of the laws governing each case, and of their proper application.

Thousands have been healed of the enslaving habits of the use of tobacco, morphine, alcohol, etc. It is claimed that insane people have been cured and their reason restored by this power. Insomnia is easily cured by its use. Sleep is nature's greatest healer. The poet says: "Nature's sweet restorer, balmy sleep." Sleep produced by narcotics leaves the system depleted. Magnetic sleep restores the wasted energies.

THE OPERATION OF THE HEAVENLY RADIO VERY SIMILAR TO THE MECHANICAL RADIO OF THIS MATERIAL WORLD, BUT FAR SUPERIOR TO IT

It requires an electric battery attached to a radio receiving instrument to make it possible for it to receive and repeat the message broadcasted by the distant operator. The human being is an electro-magnetic battery. He has all the necessary appliances of the mechanical radio of this material world and possesses much more. He is endowed with mental and Spiritual forces and faculties that transcends almost infinitely the ability of the mechanical radio. He has intelligence, knowledge of language, powers of reason, etc., and when thoughts expressed or impressed upon the mind which is the antenna or a segmented organ or sensation, he understands, while the radio only repeats the words, understanding nothing. The development of spirit mediumship is simply the learning how to adjust the mind and brain to the vibratory forces to record the message broadcasted by the heavenly messengers or operators.

Spirit mediumship is not miraculous, but like the radio is governed by natural law. The spiritual forces reach the healing medium by the heavenly radio exactly as the spirit message does, though by different rates of vibration.

### THE LAW OF PSYCHIC PHENOMENA AND SPIRIT MEDIUMSHIP

Everything in spiritual science is natural and operates under natural law.

Man is a psychic and subject to psychic law in many ways. This subject covers a great field and is little understood by a large majority of the human race, and yet it concerns every human being as much or perhaps more than any other one subject. Some people who are ignorant of its great, wonderful and universal power and activities cast it aside with some frivolous remark and with them the matter is settled. They know little or nothing of the many subjects in which the law of psychic phenomena takes a leading part.

In considering the subject we can here only mention a few of the many departments of life in which it is actively operating, though mostly without the consciousness of those through whom it is acting.

### THIS LAW ACTS IN THE PHYSICAL MAN

In the physical man psychic law acts through the brain upon the nervous system, solar plexus, and the cuticle.

### IN THE MENTAL MAN

In the mental man it operates upon every faculty of mind, consciousness, reason, will, love nature, and all others. The study of which in each case is of unbounded interest.

In the spiritual man it acts with greatest power. Psychic Law influences, often directs the action of man's religious nature, inspiration, aspiration, religious emotions, etc., and in spirit mediumship manifests its wonderful, spiritual, and most important power. It is manifesting in spirit mediumship in all its phases, physical, mental, and spiritual. The law of psychic phenomena rules in every one of the 40 phases of modern Spiritualism.

Not only is it the controlling power used by spirits in Spiritualism, but it enters into and has to do with many activities of this, our everyday life, whether we know it or not. Until we have learned this fact from the teachings of Modern Spiritualism we do not realize it, but the more we become acquainted with this great truth, the more of it is revealed to us.

Psychic Science is ever manifest in mesmerism, hypnotism, psychology, suggestive theraputics, mental and spiritual healing, etc.

In eugenics it may be used to bless if its truths and methods of application are known and properly applied. The dangers lie only in the ignorance of the law and of its proper application.

When its laws are properly understood and applied, it will become a still greater blessing to the world.

Through following the true teachings of eugenics as taught by spirits in Spiritualism, children may be properly born into this life, and we all know that every child has a perfect right to be born with a good physical body, free from any taint of disease, with a happy disposition, a skull large enough to hold his brain without pinching it. Children should be born with a full love nature and fitted to live the life of earth properly. Spiritual eugenics teaches the proper application of psychic law, to grant to every child all of these and many, many other of God's blessed inheritances. Oh, when will the world awaken to the glories of Spiritual Science as taught and demonstrated in modern Spiritualism.

To do justice to this subject we should take up one by one all the subjects touched upon here and many more showing the effects of this great law upon each mental and spiritual faculty of man. It would take much time and discussion of the subject to portray its mighty psychological influence as used in the business world alone and mostly by men who never studied the subject at all, and it is used continually in the social, political, and especially in the religious activities of the human race.

We may make ourselves happy or miserable through the action of our minds. A smile may represent love, joy, peace, and satisfaction, or a smile may carry with its influence, incredulity, sarcasm, scorn, contempt or anger, all of which are the expressions of the spirit. Thus the spirit expresses itself in different manner through smiles. So it is with every act of our lives. If our thoughts are good, they write the expression of good all over our countenance. If our thoughts are evil, they write their story in our faces, and we may transmit those facial expressions to our offspring.

Man is a soul and cannot be lost. Spiritualism has come to help him find himself. He is not lost, he is here, but he has not yet found his entire self.

Man being subject to this law and at the same time ignorant of the fact that there is such a law, and that it has any influence upon him, he makes many mistakes. Therefore, for his own good he must become familiar with this law of soul or spirit. We are souls or spirits and all expressions of ours that we send out, whether they are clothed with words, gestures, smiles, frowns, or only sent by the power of thought, return to bless or curse us. We reap what we sow. We have spiritual faculties heretofore unknown and unexplained. Spiritualism has come to explain them, to develop them and to acquaint mankind with the psychic laws governing the race.

Evil and ugly thoughts are blocks under the wheels of progression in the development of Spirit mediumship. Good thoughts, happy thoughts, loving thoughts, aspiring for good, and praying for it, are helpers along the way of development of good, and making the conditions for spiritual unfoldment and of good health.

Oh, dear mediums, listen faithfully to your spirit friends, live good lives, think good thoughts, pray for guidance, follow spirit direction, avoid anger, hatred and all unpleasant thoughts. Live in a happy vibration, trust your spirit guides. Devote your lives to the sacred mission you are performing. God and angels bless you as they have and still are blessing me.

### EVERY MAN, THE RULER OF HIS OWN DESTINY

"There is no chance, no destiny, no fate
  Can circumvent, or hinder, or control
  The firm resolve of a determined soul.
Gifts count for little; will alone is great.
All things give way before it, soon or late.
Conquer we shall, but we must first contend;
  'Tis not the fight that crowns, it is the end."

—Anon

### NOTHING IMPOSSIBLE WITH GOD

"There is nothing impossible with God," says the Christian. Jesus said: "Ye are Gods."

This is Bible and if true, there is nothing impossible with man. Anyway we will say: There is no limit to the possibilities of men. The child is the repository of infinite possibilities, said Andrew Jackson Davis, the first Modern Spiritualist. Beautiful thought! What a source of optimism and of inspiration this thought should be to every one. Why then should man grovel on the low plains of fear, hatred, jealousy, etc.?

### BORROWED TROUBLE

It is true that borrowed trouble produces real trouble.

### FEAR

Fear of sickness often produces sickness. One who is afraid of sickness, of contagious diseases, is more liable to take them. Fear is the curse of men.

Why, people brooding over things they fear may happen, are sometimes led to commit suicide. Fear and borrowed trouble have often wrought such havoc upon the plastic and receptive mind that the poor victims could not wait until the feared calamity came, but killed themselves before for fear it might come. In the time of the late world war a newspaper report was published stating that a man and his wife killed themselves because they feared he would be drafted into the army. Fear caused their deaths. Borrowed trouble took their lives. If they had understood the laws of psychic phenomena and applied them they would probably have been living and well today.

To change the conditions of trouble and discouragement, quit thinking that kind of thoughts. Think thoughts of joy, happy thoughts, sing jolly songs, whistle lively tunes, crack jokes, and dance a jig, and determine in your own mind that you will not live in an atmosphere of despondency and analyze carefully your many blessings, prayerfully thanking the giver of them all. Forget the little things that annoy and trouble you, and remember the things you enjoy. It is easy to do.

### NATURAL LAW IN THE PSYCHIC REALMS

Natural law prevails in the psychic realms of both worlds. We do our thinking under this law. We are privileged to choose our lines of thinking. Nature pays everyone in his own coin. If we smile, nature smiles on us in return. If we frown, we may think we are frowned upon. Think well and you attract thinkers. If you love the world, you will reap a harvest of love and goodness.

Failure sometimes pays better than success. It is a teacher, therefore not always a calamity. Do not look for trouble, for if you do you will surely find it. Worry often acts as advance agent for the undertaker.

### EVERY MAN A RULER OF HIS OWN DESTINY— A KING OF HIS OWN EMPIRE

Every normal man may become a ruler or a slave. Every human being is a spiritual entity, and may become, yea! should become the ruler of his own destiny. He has entire charge of his own physical organism. He is responsible for its care and condition. He, by his will, may place it in jeopardy, or he may care for it properly. Every normal man is responsible to himself for the proper care and condition of the human form in which he dwells, barring unavoidable accidents, epidemics, etc.

Man is the sovereign ruler of his own empire, the human body, for this reason, he should understand its construction, and the laws governing and controlling it. This includes the physical, mental, and moral, as well as the psychical or spiritual man, because the psychic laws affect the physical, mental, and spiritual man, in every way.

Man is a creature of inheritance of circumstances and environment; but he is a creator and creates new environment, new circumstances, and may outgrow and overcome undesirable inheritances.

Man is the natural ruler of his own empire, his body and mind, and should prepare himself thoroughly by careful study of the laws governing his entire being.

If we study man in his moods, his passions, ambitions, hopes, aspirations, religious views, and in his idiosyncracies, we will find him to be a wonderful combination. The spirit of man is not an organ of the body nor the spiritual body, but it permeates, animates and uses all the organs of both the physical body and the spiritual body. The organs of the body are man's subjects. He should get acquainted with each one of them, learning well their missions, that he may co-operate with them in ruling and governing his whole empire.

"Man, know thyself" are the golden words, fraught with great meaning. Our advice to everyone must be: Think well of yourself. Have confidence in yourself. Believe in yourself. Be yourself, aping no man. Aim high. Plan for great things. Nothing is too great for you to reach. All is advancement. All is progression, evolution is the law of nature. Get into the swells and you will reach the harbor on the crest of the waves.

Look not for the weaknesses and mistakes of others, but seek to learn their strength and attainments. Seek the good in everything and you will be in heaven at once, and without leaving this world or dying.

Modern spiritualism is the true savior of the world. It is God's latest revelation to mankind. Its message is better understood than any ancient revelation, because man knows more about natural law, psychic law and *nature's divine revelations* than was known by

our ancestors when these same spiritual phenomena we are receiving to-day came to them.

### THEN AND NOW

There's many things revealed to-day
  That came to men in ancient times,
Then undevelopment held sway.
  As knowledge grows error declines.

Our forefathers made great mistakes
  In their interpretations, see?
Like men to-day, who undertake
  To know God and eternity.

We know but little more 'tis true;
  But that little, to us, is great,
It solves death's problems to the few
  Who seek, and truths investigate.

That little does *well prove this fact*:
  Life after death for all mankind,
Which adds to faith, and holds intact
  *This truth*, to which some men are blind.

Oh, what a blessing! This relieves
  The doubts, the fears, and clears the way
As those who *know*—more than *believe*—
  But *all shall know this truth some day.*

Spiritual healing is a natural faculty and as common to the people as music or art, but mankind has been deprived of the knowledge of its possession as a natural faculty and taught from childhood for centuries that it was a special gift from God and only given to a few chosen prophets of the Bible centuries ago.

But when Modern Spiritualism came to the world and communion with the so-called dead was established in the year 1848, the spirits revived the practice of healing by laying on of hands, and taught those that were willing to listen to them that such healing was a natural faculty of the human race; and they taught the Spiritualists the philosophy, the science, and the religion of healing by laying on of hands. The Christians in the early years of Christianity practiced it, but later abandoned it. Yet always claiming to be the true followers of Jesus, though apparently forgetting that Jesus said: John XVI, 12: "He that believeth on me the works that I do shall he do also, and greater works than these shall he do because I go unto my Father."

Mark XVI, 17: "And these signs shall follow them that believe. In my name shall they cast out devils, they shall speak with new tongues." 18th verse: "They shall take up serpents and if they drink any deadly thing it shall not hurt them. *They shall lay hands on the sick and they shall recover.*"

We Spiritualists speak in tongues and lay hands on the sick and they do recover. The other things mentioned here they do not dare try to do. Then, who are the believers, who are fulfilling the prophecy of the noble man of Nazareth? Spiritualism has analyzed the methods of Spiritual healing and discovered to the world that it is not a miracle as taught by orthodox Christianity. It has proved that the philosophy of healing by laying on of hands is natural and it has taught and practiced it for four-score years with the greatest success though under very adverse conditions, because of what Jesus emphasized as lack of faith, and of unbelief. However, the practice of healing by laying on of hands by Spiritualists has converted many thousands of Christians to this truth that their savior taught and practiced, and many denominations of Christianity are taking it up of late and giving it different names, some of whom appear very anxious to have the people think that they are not imitating the Spiritualists.

Spiritualists teach and practice the science and natural philosophy of healing by laying on of hands and with great success, and that is the leading purpose of this book. May it cause many to investigate and make the test of their powers, and to develop them becoming efficient spiritual healers and blessing the world by healing the sick, and replacing happiness for misery, ease for disease, and health for sickness, while aiding the people of this world in the knowledge of the laws and the blessing of Magnetic, Mental and Spiritual healing is the sincere prayer of the author.

### DOES EVIL AID PROGRESSION?
### DO WE LEARN BY OUR MISTAKES?

Evil thoughts lead to evil deeds. Good thoughts are powerful aids to good deeds. It is one of man's many blessings that he can know that he makes mistakes, and that he may learn from them; and also that he has the power to correct and outgrow them in this life if he wills to do it.

The truth continues in the spirit world and the Spiritualists teach that "The door to reformation is never closed against any human soul, either here or hereafter."

Man's mistakes when rectified and outgrown lead on toward perfection. This being true, proves that our mistakes may be made useful in our advancement. Furthermore; it may be said—Evil is a teacher from which man may learn by contrasting it with good which is best for him, and sometime, somewhere, when he has learned which is best for him, he may be able to choose the good and be good, working out his own salvation.

Is evil undeveloped good? Gen. Chap. 1, verse 31: "God saw everything that he had made, and, behold, it was very good."

IS THIS DEAR OLD WORLD ALL FOR ME?

This dear old world's a lovely one,
  And the things in it I see

Are all complete, the work well done,
  And were they made for me?

The architect with good effect
  Planned the beauties that I see;
He made it all into a ball
  And rolls it now for me.

It's wonderful to look upon
  And to breathe its pure air free,
When it is known one's not alone
  And all was made for me.

The stars by night are my delight,
  Their brilliancy I see
They furnish light for moonless night
  Just think it's all for me.

I'm a proud one because the sun
  Shines on o'er land and sea,
And here is one whose thought has come
  To know it's all for me.

I love the laws and praise the Cause
  Whatever it may be,
For He is good, that's understood,
  Who made it all for me.

In the financial world men are looking for good investments, and when a man makes a bad investment it usually brings him a lesson by which he profits. He becomes more careful and seeks to avoid poor investments in the future. In this it may be seen that what seems an unprofitable financial investment may sometimes prove a good investment in the long run, as the experience may save him money, because he will refrain from bad investments and be more likely to make good ones. Experience though dearly bought is, no doubt, the best teacher.

Instead of borrowing trouble as most people do we should learn to *borrow happiness, pleasure,* and those things that bring us harmony because harmony is the foundation principle of health, happiness and heaven.

It is easier and certainly better to borrow pleasure than pain or trouble. Don't worry. Borrowed trouble kills people and is indeed a poor investment. It never pays dividends or a per cent on the investment. It is sure to prove a failure. The right kind of borrowing is a great lever fulcrum in business. Harmony breeds happiness. My advice would be to all, *Borrow Happiness* and it will prove a paying stroke of business. It will pay two hundred per cent on the investment and is guaranteed at that. Why do we not invest more in these guaranteed securities? It is because we are not properly informed regarding the interest and dividends they are paying. Why do we continue to make bad investments by purchasing at such enormous cost *trouble that never comes?* Borrowed trouble is lived over and over again ad infinitum, but real trouble—when experienced—passes away. There comes usually an end of it, a final passing, and its results are accepted. There is so much more borrowed trouble than real trouble in the world that real trouble appears insignificant in comparison, because borrowed trouble is continuous, never ending. We worry and fret about the weather; for fear we miss the train; that the children may catch cold; etc. In fact, we borrow trouble about nearly everything and make mountains out of mole-hills at that.

Prophesying evil or borrowing trouble is bad for one's health and happiness. It tears down tissue as it is a powerful suggestive force and leads to real trouble, bringing on sickness, insanity and other ills.

We should learn to enjoy our blessings. They are too numerous to mention and I question if one of us could begin now and enumerate them all.

One who is blessed with eyesight, or hearing, powers of speech, smell, tastes or feeling, or whose mind is clear, whose power to think and reason is still retained is blessed indeed above those who have lost any one of these beautiful faculties. It is indeed wrong for one to fret, worry, find fault, or become despondent who is in possession of his faculties and is in reasonably good health. If one has the habit of borrowing trouble or looking upon the dark side of life he can and should begin at once to break up the habit and come out into the radiant brightness and harmonious vibrations that the consciousness of these many other blessings brings to those who have learned to live the happy life.

Let us each one resolve to make the very best of everything and live the happy life, borrowing no trouble, crossing no bridges until we reach them, and thus making heaven here and now for ourselves and our associates. Living a harmonious life creates vibrations of health and happiness.

### HOW TO BECOME HEALTHY AND HAPPY

But, says someone, how can I do it? It is easy when your mind is made up to do it. First, put away every unpleasant thought and count your blessings. Dwell upon the good things you possess and should enjoy. If you are in the habit of borrowing trouble, stop it. You can control your thought if you determine to do it. If you are subject to despondency, commence to whistle and sing, and if that does not relieve you, get out into the middle of the floor and dance a jig, and continue to dance until the perspiration rolls off your body. Think of the fun you have had. Will yourself to have more. Study the beauty of nature, analyze the lovely flowers and don't allow yourself to think an evil thought or a thought of trouble. And ask your best beloved spirit friends to help you while you do your best to help yourself.

Go to the quiet of your room alone a few minutes each day. Mentally ask your spirit loved ones to listen to your thoughts, then think over the failures you have made in trying to overcome borrowing trouble, then change the thought vibration by thinking of the success you have made in putting away evil thoughts and borrowing trouble and ask your best beloved spirit friends to help you in continuing the good efforts. Then make new resolves and go forth with stronger determination to smile and rejoice, and sing and be happy, and in a little time it will become second nature to you, and you will be well and happy.

### DOING GOOD RESULTS IN GOOD TO THE DOER

"In the effort to do good one cultivates his own Soul. In the cultivation of soul one develops health."

Soul culture generates health and happiness. We should get these facts well established in our minds. We have only to make the conditions nature demands to accomplish any natural result. Cause and effect are the inexorable law of nature. The more pure and refined one becomes the greater will be his powers which clearly explains the fact that the better life we live, the better healer or medium for any phase we may become.

### A LESSON ON HEALTH AND HAPPINESS.
### AFFIRMATIONS

As I am the ruler of my own empire (my body) I am responsible for the conditions prevailing within its borders; therefore I will go at once about the work of putting things to rights within the borders of my domain.

From this moment I will change the vibration of my being. I am entitled to good health and to happiness. These are my natural inheritances. I am endowed with the ability to become healthy and happy and *I will be happy. I will not be sick. I will be well. My vital forces shall increase.* I am getting stronger every day. My vital forces are increasing, I am better now. I will not become angry, because anger and evil thinking exhausts my vitality, tears down tissue, destroys health and makes me unhappy. I will be well. I am well.

ON RETIRING AT NIGHT

On retiring at night I will affirm with confidence as follows: I am feeling better tonight, I will improve in health and strength while I sleep and shall awaken in the morning refreshed and feeling well. Dear spirit friends, help me to be firm and to carry out this determination.

### MORNING AFFIRMATION

On awakening each morning I will rejoice at the morning's dawn. My heart shall be glad and my spirit shall be full of joy and thankfulness because I am alive. I am well. I am happy. I will do everything I can to-day to be happy and to make others happy. Beloved spirit friends, help me to fulfil this resolve, and bring to me your wonderful healing forces if I fulfil this pledge on my part. Oh, how happy I am in the knowledge of your presence, your love and assistance. You are such a wonderful blessing to me.

I will try to love everyone throughout this beautiful day, friends and enemies, if I have enemies.

Our friends bring us strength and our enemies need help, that they may become free from the evil thoughts that possess them and when they are free from them they must also become our friends. I will think for them only good thoughts. I will not allow myself to express an ugly or evil word. I will speak only pleasant and kindly words throughout this blessed day. I will be good and do good, the dear spirit friends helping me, and this will make me happy and keep me well.

This kind of thinking and doing will keep me in good health, and greatly help in the development of my mediumship and make me and my friends happy, while fitting me for the important duties of life, and will add years to my life on earth.

The sincere and conscientious practice and application of these affirmations changes burdens to pleasures, sorrows to joys, sickness to health, and unhappiness to happiness.

## TRUTH FOR AUTHORITY AND REASON
### AS ITS INTERPRETER

*An Axiom of Modern Spiritualism*

Oh Truth! Thou Savior of the world!
  Thy glory shineth everywhere,
Thy banner true to all unfurled
  Thy blessings everyone may share.

Thou'rt not hid nor esoteric,
  But ever present to our view,
Always thou art exoteric
  Dispensing facts both old and new.

Oh, Truth! If thou but governed all
  And hand in hand walked with true love,
No human soul would ever fall
  All wrong each one would live above.

Earth would be a heaven's bower,
  All men like angels might become
Clothed with spiritual power
  While living in the earthly home.

Let's seek the *Truth* though shattered be
  Our idols worshipped all these years;
Let's follow *Truth* until we see
  The last of all our pain and tears.

Oh, Reason, Truth, with Love combined!
    Thy magic power is not concealed;
A trinity of the divine,
    In thee to mankind is revealed.

All hail, the *Truth*! From day to day
    It clearer comes to mortal view,
And knowing *Truth* just lights the way,
    Helping mankind to live more true.

May the dear spirits from above
    Help us this trinity to know
That all mankind in peace and love
    May dwell on earth and when they go

To spheres of light where angels dwell
    May each have filled his mission here,
That with all there it may be well,
    For *Truth* reigns in that higher sphere.

### SPIRITUALISM OF THE CHRISTIAN BIBLE

The Christian Bible teaches Spiritualism though few Christians know it. The fundamental teachings of Jesus of Nazareth are Spiritualism as recorded in the New Testament. He taught Spiritualism and demonstrated its truths by his mediumship.

Spiritualism embodies the fundamental teachings of the early Christian religion.

There should be no controversy between Christians and Spiritualists, and will be none when Christians learn the true teachings of the New Testament Scriptures, as explained by Spiritualism.

To understand the Christian Bible read the following named books:

## "Was Jesus of Nazareth God or Man, Christ or Spirit Medium?"

### LET THE BIBLE DECIDE

This book amply proves by the Scriptures that Jesus of Nazareth was born of earthly parents as are other children. The testimony of Matthew, Mark, Luke, John, Peter, and of Jesus Himself declares it. The Scriptures themselves plainly show that He was a wonderful Spirit Medium possessing both the mental and physical phases; that His parents were both mediums, that He had a large band of Spirit guides or guardians; that He was an Inspirational Speaker; a Test Medium; a

Medium for Spirit Voices; a Mind Reader; that He gave private readings; was a Trance Medium, and a Materializing Medium. And that He taught Spiritualism and demonstrated its truth by the exercising of His own Mediumship.

It is a book of 180 pages, is neatly bound in cloth, embossed in gold, and contains a good portrait of the author. Price, postage paid, $2.00.

## "All the Spiritualism of the Christian Bible, and the Scripture Directly Opposing it."

### ALSO THE MATERIALISM OF THE BIBLE PROPHETS

Let us take the Bible at its real, true value, but not at the estimate of fanatics.

This book is indeed a Revelation. It is a New and Scientific Interpretation of these Scriptures. It contains an index of 1,052 Bible references, hundreds of which teach the phenomena, science and religion of Spiritualism. This index also enables one to turn at once to Bible records of any phase of Mediumship or phenomena, such as "spirit slate writing," "spirit materialization," "trumpet speaking," "clairvoyance," clairaudience," "impersonation," "impressional Mediumship" and nearly all of the forty mental and physical phases of Mediumship of Modern Spiritualism.

All of the Scripture directly opposing Spiritualism is quoted, as are many passages which teach materialism—the terrible doctrine that death ends all.

This book is a new revelation of the teachings of the Bible and makes clear parts of it that heretofore seemed impossible to understand. It is a great help in explaining Spiritualism to Bible believers, and is a powerful weapon of defense in the hands of Spiritualists when attacked by its Christian opponents.

It is a thought producer and records facts for hundreds of sermons and lectures, and in fact it is a text book needed in the study and teaching of Modern Spiritualism.

It quotes many hundreds of Scripture passages that teach Spiritualism, and is a complete text book of the Spiritualism of the Bible. This book has 392 pages, contains a good portrait of the author, and is neatly bound in cloth and embossed in gold.

Price, postage paid, $4.00.

Address: REV. E. W. SPRAGUE

621 Madison Avenue, S. E.

Grand Rapids, Mich.

# CHRISTMAS FUN

# MADLIBS®

By Roger Price and Leonard Stern

Mad Libs
An Imprint of Penguin Random House

MAD LIBS
An Imprint of Penguin Random House LLC, New York

Concept created by Roger Price & Leonard Stern

Published by Mad Libs,
an imprint of Penguin Random House LLC, New York.
Printed in the USA.

Visit us online at www.penguinrandomhouse.com.

ISBN 9780843112382
35 37 39 40 38 36

MAD LIBS is a registered trademark of Penguin Random House LLC.

# MAD LIBS

# INSTRUCTIONS

MAD LIBS® is a game for people who don't like games!
It can be played by one, two, three, four, or forty.

## • RIDICULOUSLY SIMPLE DIRECTIONS

In this tablet you will find stories containing blank spaces where words
are left out. One player, the READER, selects one of these stories. The
READER does not tell anyone what the story is about. Instead, he/she asks
the other players, the WRITERS, to give him/her words. These words are
used to fill in the blank spaces in the story.

## • TO PLAY

The READER asks each WRITER in turn to call out a word—an adjective or
a noun or whatever the space calls for—and uses them to fill in the blank
spaces in the story. The result is a MAD LIBS® game.

When the READER then reads the completed MAD LIBS® game to the other
players, they will discover that they have written a story that is fantastic,
screamingly funny, shocking, silly, crazy, or just plain dumb—depending
upon which words each WRITER called out.

## • EXAMPLE (*Before* and *After*)

"_____!" he said _____
      EXCLAMATION                ADVERB

as he jumped into his convertible _____ and
                                           NOUN

drove off with his _____ wife.
                      ADJECTIVE

"**OUCH**_____!" he said **HAPPILY**_____
      EXCLAMATION                ADVERB

as he jumped into his convertible **CAT**_____ and
                                           NOUN

drove off with his **BRAVE**_____ wife.
                      ADJECTIVE

In case you have forgotten what adjectives, adverbs, nouns, and verbs are, here is a quick review:

An ADJECTIVE describes something or somebody. *Lumpy, soft, ugly, messy,* and *short* are adjectives.

An ADVERB tells how something is done. It modifies a verb and usually ends in "ly." *Modestly, stupidly, greedily,* and *carefully* are adverbs.

A NOUN is the name of a person, place or thing. *Sidewalk, umbrella, bridle, bathtub,* and *nose* are nouns.

A VERB is an action word. *Run, pitch, jump,* and *swim* are verbs. Put the verbs in past tense if the directions say PAST TENSE. *Ran, pitched, jumped,* and *swam* are verbs in the past tense.

When we ask for A PLACE, we mean any sort of place: a country or city *(Spain, Cleveland)* or a room *(bathroom, kitchen.)*

An EXCLAMATION or SILLY WORD is any sort of funny sound, gasp, grunt, or outcry, like *Wow!, Ouch!, Whomp!, Ick!,* and *Gadzooks!*

When we ask for specific words, like a NUMBER, a COLOR, an ANIMAL, or a PART OF THE BODY, we mean a word that is one of those things, like *seven, blue, horse,* or *head.*

When we ask for a PLURAL, it means more than one. For example, *cat* pluralized is *cats.*

MAD LIBS® is fun to play with friends, but you can also play it by yourself! To begin with, DO NOT look at the story on the page below. Fill in the blanks on this page with the words called for. Then, using the words you have selected, fill in the blank spaces in the story.

Now you've created your own hilarious MAD LIBS® game!

# SELECTING A TREE

ADJECTIVE_____

ADJECTIVE_____

ROOM _____

PLURAL NOUN _____

PLURAL NOUN _____

NOUN _____

NOUN _____

NOUN _____

ADJECTIVE_____

NOUN _____

NUMBER _____

PLURAL NOUN _____

NOUN _____

COLOR_____

ANOTHER COLOR _____

SOMETHING ALIVE _____

PERSON IN ROOM _____

ANOTHER PERSON IN ROOM _____

# MAD LIBS

# SELECTING A TREE

No Christmas season can be really _____ unless you have
ADJECTIVE

a/an _____ tree in your _____. If you live in
ADJECTIVE           ROOM

a city, you will see many vacant _____ filled with hundreds
PLURAL NOUN

of _____ for sale. If you live in the country, you can get
PLURAL NOUN

your own _____ right out of the forest. Go out with a/an
NOUN

_____ and _____, and when you see a/an _____
NOUN       NOUN           ADJECTIVE

tree you like, you can dig it up and plant it in a/an _____.
NOUN

Then you can use it for _____ years. To make sure your tree
NUMBER

is fresh, shake the branches and see if the _____ fall off onto
PLURAL NOUN

the _____. And make sure the tree is very _____.
NOUN           COLOR

Nothing looks worse than a/an _____ tree. Just follow these
ANOTHER COLOR

directions and you can have a perfectly beautiful _____ in
SOMETHING ALIVE

your front room for weeks. Remember, poems and Mad Libs are made

by fools like _____, but only _____
PERSON IN ROOM           ANOTHER PERSON IN ROOM

can make a tree.

From CHRISTMAS FUN MAD LIBS® • Copyright © 2001, 1985 by Penguin Random House LLC.

MAD LIBS® is fun to play with friends, but you can also play it by yourself! To begin with, DO NOT look at the story on the page below. Fill in the blanks on this page with the words called for. Then, using the words you have selected, fill in the blank spaces in the story.

Now you've created your own hilarious MAD LIBS® game!

# DECORATING THE TREE

NOUN _____

PERSON IN ROOM _____

ADJECTIVE_____

VERB _____

ANOTHER PERSON IN ROOM _____

PLURAL NOUN _____

ANOTHER PERSON IN ROOM _____

TYPE OF FOOD (PLURAL) _____

ANOTHER TYPE OF FOOD (PLURAL) _____

PLURAL NOUN _____

ADJECTIVE_____

ADJECTIVE_____

PLURAL NOUN _____

ADJECTIVE_____

NOUN _____

ADJECTIVE_____

ADJECTIVE_____

NOUN _____

PLURAL NOUN _____

NOUN _____

EXCLAMATION_____

# MAD LIBS®
# DECORATING THE TREE

Many people decorate their Christmas _____ on Christmas
NOUN

Eve. Last year _____ had a/an _____ party
PERSON IN ROOM        ADJECTIVE

and everyone helped _____ the tree. _____
VERB        ANOTHER PERSON IN ROOM

brought tinsel and _____. And _____ brought
PLURAL NOUN        ANOTHER PERSON IN ROOM

lots of fresh _____ and candy _____
TYPE OF FOOD (PLURAL)        ANOTHER TYPE OF FOOD (PLURAL)

to put on the tree. The most important decoration, of course, is the

string of colored electric _____. A few dozen _____
PLURAL NOUN        ADJECTIVE

lights make any tree look _____. And most stores sell
ADJECTIVE

round, sparkly _____ and little _____ balls to
PLURAL NOUN        ADJECTIVE

hang on the branches. But the hardest decoration to pick is the one

that goes right on top. Once that _____ is up, you know
NOUN

that the _____ season has officially started. Of course, if
ADJECTIVE

you are too _____ to have a tree for Christmas, you can
ADJECTIVE

decorate your _____ or hang _____ on your
NOUN        PLURAL NOUN

_____. Then the neighbors will say, "_____!"
NOUN        EXCLAMATION

From CHRISTMAS FUN MAD LIBS® • Copyright © 2001, 1985 by Penguin Random House LLC.

MAD LIBS® is fun to play with friends, but you can also play it by yourself! To begin with, DO NOT look at the story on the page below. Fill in the blanks on this page with the words called for. Then, using the words you have selected, fill in the blank spaces in the story.

Now you've created your own hilarious MAD LIBS® game!

# HOW TO WRAP A PRESENT

_____ ADJECTIVE

_____ PLURAL NOUN

_____ ADJECTIVE

_____ SOMETHING BIG

_____ SOMETHING SOFT

_____ VERB

_____ NOUN

_____ ADVERB

_____ SOMETHING SHARP

_____ COLOR

_____ NOUN

_____ ADJECTIVE

_____ VERB

_____ ADJECTIVE

_____ PLURAL NOUN

_____ ADJECTIVE

_____ EXCLAMATION

_____ ADJECTIVE

# MAD LIBS®
# HOW TO WRAP A PRESENT

Before you start to wrap your Christmas present, make sure you have

plenty of _____ paper and lots of little _____ to
           ADJECTIVE                             PLURAL NOUN

stick on the package. If you are wrapping something _____,
                                                     ADJECTIVE

such as a/an _____, it is best to tape _____
                SOMETHING BIG                       SOMETHING SOFT

around any parts that might _____. Then take brown
                                  VERB

wrapping _____ and wrap it very_____. Take
            NOUN                          ADVERB

care that there is not a/an _____ poking out anywhere.
                            SOMETHING SHARP

Now take the expensive _____ paper that you bought at the
                            COLOR

_____ store and make a/an _____ package. Finally,
    NOUN                          ADJECTIVE

put stickers on that say, "Do not _____ until Christmas"
                                VERB

and put it under the tree with all of the other _____
                                         ADJECTIVE

_____. Then on Christmas morning, when you see all of
  PLURAL NOUN

your _____ relatives opening their packages and saying,
        ADJECTIVE

"_____!" you will feel positively _____.
    EXCLAMATION                               ADJECTIVE

From CHRISTMAS FUN MAD LIBS® • Copyright © 2001, 1985 by Penguin Random House LLC.

MAD LIBS® is fun to play with friends, but you can also play it by yourself! To begin with, DO NOT look at the story on the page below. Fill in the blanks on this page with the words called for. Then, using the words you have selected, fill in the blank spaces in the story.

Now you've created your own hilarious MAD LIBS® game!

# WHAT TO GET PEOPLE FOR CHRISTMAS

ADJECTIVE _____

ADJECTIVE _____

PLURAL NOUN _____

NOUN _____

NOUN _____

ADJECTIVE _____

NOUN _____

VERB _____

NOUN _____

ROOM _____

VERB _____

PLURAL NOUN _____

COLOR _____

ARTICLE OF CLOTHING _____

TYPE OF ACTIVITY _____

PERSON IN ROOM (FEMALE) _____

ANOTHER ARTICLE OF CLOTHING _____

CELEBRITY _____

PERSON IN ROOM (MALE) _____

PLURAL NOUN _____

PART OF THE BODY _____

NOUN _____

# MAD LIBS®
## WHAT TO GET PEOPLE
## FOR CHRISTMAS

One of the _____ things about Christmas is being able
                ADJECTIVE

to pick out _____ presents to give to your _____
              ADJECTIVE                                    PLURAL NOUN

and relatives. But it's a problem because you don't want to give some-

one a/an _____ when they really wanted a/an _____.
            NOUN                                          NOUN

Here are some _____ gift ideas. I bet your mother would
                  ADJECTIVE

like a new electric _____ she could use to _____
                        NOUN                                 VERB

her vegetables or clean the _____ in the _____.
                                NOUN              ROOM

If your father likes to _____, he could use a new set of
                            VERB

_____. Or a/an _____ all-wool _____
PLURAL NOUN                    COLOR              ARTICLE OF CLOTHING

while he is playing _____. If you want to get
                        TYPE OF ACTIVITY

_____ a present, she needs a sports
        PERSON IN ROOM (FEMALE)

_____ designed by _____. And
ANOTHER ARTICLE OF CLOTHING                 CELEBRITY

_____ needs some _____ to keep his
PERSON IN ROOM (MALE)                       PLURAL NOUN

_____ warm. But no matter what you give, remember it
PART OF THE BODY

is the _____ behind the gift that counts.
          NOUN

MAD LIBS® is fun to play with friends, but you can also play it by yourself! To begin with, DO NOT look at the story on the page below. Fill in the blanks on this page with the words called for. Then, using the words you have selected, fill in the blank spaces in the story.

Now you've created your own hilarious MAD LIBS® game!

## CHRISTMAS DINNER

ADJECTIVE _____

TYPE OF BIRD _____

TYPE OF FOOD _____

PLURAL NOUN _____

TYPE OF LIQUID _____

ADJECTIVE _____

VERB _____

NOUN _____

PART OF THE BODY _____

TYPE OF CONTAINER _____

ADJECTIVE _____

NOUN _____

NUMBER _____

ADVERB _____

ADJECTIVE _____

PLURAL NOUN _____

EXCLAMATION _____

# MAD LIBS®
# CHRISTMAS DINNER

Everyone likes to have a/an _____ dinner on Christmas
ADJECTIVE

Day. Most people have a huge roast _____ stuffed with
TYPE OF BIRD

_____ dressing and served with mashed _____
TYPE OF FOOD                                                    PLURAL NOUN

and plenty of hot brown _____. However, if you would
TYPE OF LIQUID

rather have a/an _____ turkey, here is how you should
ADJECTIVE

_____ it. First, make the dressing of old, dried _____
VERB                                                              NOUN

crumbs. Then, put the dressing in the turkey's _____.
PART OF THE BODY

Put it in a big _____ and brush it with _____
TYPE OF CONTAINER                                    ADJECTIVE

butter. Next, heat your _____ to _____ degrees.
NOUN                              NUMBER

Put the turkey in and cook it very _____ for five hours.
ADVERB

When you put it on the table, the _____ aroma will make
ADJECTIVE

everyone smack their _____ and say, " _____ !"
PLURAL NOUN                          EXCLAMATION

MAD LIBS® is fun to play with friends, but you can also play it by yourself! To begin with, DO NOT look at the story on the page below. Fill in the blanks on this page with the words called for. Then, using the words you have selected, fill in the blank spaces in the story.

Now you've created your own hilarious MAD LIBS® game!

# TOYS FOR THE KIDS

ADJECTIVE _____

PLURAL NOUN _____

ADJECTIVE _____

SILLY WORD _____

PLURAL NOUN _____

NUMBER _____

VERB _____

LETTER OF THE ALPHABET _____

PLURAL NOUN _____

NOUN _____

ANIMAL _____

NOUN _____

NOUN _____

ADJECTIVE _____

ADJECTIVE _____

ADJECTIVE _____

PLURAL NOUN _____

# MAD LIBS
## TOYS FOR THE KIDS

Today's parents buy very _____ toys for their little
                              ADJECTIVE

_____. Fifty years ago, children got _____
     PLURAL NOUN                                         ADJECTIVE

electric trains or baby dolls that said, "_____," when you
                                            SILLY WORD

squeezed them. Now children only want electronic _____.
                                                    PLURAL NOUN

Even _____-year-olds know how to _____ a computer.
        NUMBER                          VERB

Or a/an _____-Phone. Kids want remote-
          LETTER OF THE ALPHABET

controlled _____. Or tiny robot monsters that can blow
              PLURAL NOUN

up your _____ or take your _____ prisoner.
            NOUN                        ANIMAL

Everything has to have a silicon _____ in it and be operated
                                      NOUN

by a nine-volt _____. By the year 2030, all American children
                  NOUN

will probably want to have their own _____ space shuttle
                                          ADJECTIVE

and_____ robot playmate manufactured by General
      ADJECTIVE

Motors. In fact, by that time maybe children will be manufactured by

a/an _____ assembly line and will be operated by nine-volt
        ADJECTIVE

_____.
   PLURAL NOUN

MAD LIBS® is fun to play with friends, but you can also play it by yourself! To begin with, DO NOT look at the story on the page below. Fill in the blanks on this page with the words called for. Then, using the words you have selected, fill in the blank spaces in the story.

Now you've created your own hilarious MAD LIBS® game!

# A LETTER TO SANTA

_____ PERSON IN ROOM

_____ NOUN

_____ ADJECTIVE

_____ VERB

_____ EXCLAMATION

_____ VERB (PAST TENSE)

_____ VERB (PAST TENSE)

_____ PLURAL NOUN

_____ ADJECTIVE

_____ NOUN

_____ ADJECTIVE

_____ TYPE OF GAME

_____ ANOTHER PERSON IN ROOM

_____ ADJECTIVE

_____ ADJECTIVE

_____ ARTICLE OF CLOTHING

# MAD LIBS
# A LETTER TO SANTA

Dear Santa,

My name is _____, and all year I have been a very, very
        PERSON IN ROOM

good _____. I have been _____ at school, and
        NOUN                           ADJECTIVE

when my teacher asked me to _____ the whiteboard, I just
                                VERB

said, "_____!" I have not _____
        EXCLAMATION                      VERB (PAST TENSE)

or _____. Not even once. And I have helped a lot
    VERB (PAST TENSE)

of old _____ cross the street. Because I have been so
        PLURAL NOUN

_____, I am sure you are going to bring me a brand-new
ADJECTIVE

_____ with _____ wheels. I would also like to
    NOUN                ADJECTIVE

have a/an _____ racket. And a secret microphone so I can
            NOUN

spy on _____ and learn all his/her _____ secrets.
        PERSON IN ROOM                          ADJECTIVE

Well, Santa, I know you will put all these _____ presents in
                                            ADJECTIVE

my _____ on Christmas. Or else I will have been
        ARTICLE OF CLOTHING

good for nothing.

From CHRISTMAS FUN MAD LIBS® • Copyright © 2001, 1985 by Penguin Random House LLC.

MAD LIBS® is fun to play with friends, but you can also play it by yourself! To begin with, DO NOT look at the story on the page below. Fill in the blanks on this page with the words called for. Then, using the words you have selected, fill in the blank spaces in the story.

Now you've created your own hilarious MAD LIBS® game!

# A VISIT WITH SANTA AT THE NORTH POLE

_____ ADJECTIVE

_____ SOMETHING WHITE

_____ NAME OF PERSON (FEMALE)

_____ ADJECTIVE

_____ NUMBER

_____ PLURAL NOUN

_____ PLURAL NOUN

_____ TYPE OF VEHICLE

_____ ADJECTIVE

_____ ANIMAL (PLURAL)

_____ PART OF THE HOUSE

_____ NOUN

_____ ARTICLE OF CLOTHING (PLURAL)

_____ NUMBER

_____ HOLIDAY

# MAD LIBS

# A VISIT WITH SANTA
# AT THE NORTH POLE

Santa Claus has a very _____ life. He lives at the North
                              ADJECTIVE

Pole surrounded by snow and _____. He is married
                                   PLURAL NOUN

to _____ Claus and instead of children, they have
      FIRST NAME (FEMALE)

_____ little elves. This way, Santa can get help in his
      ADJECTIVE

workshop for only _____ dollars an hour. The elves work eleven
                        NUMBER

months a year making _____ and _____
                            PLURAL NOUN                PLURAL NOUN

for Santa to give children on Christmas. On Christmas Eve, the

elves load up Santa's _____ with the _____
                            VEHICLE                    ADJECTIVE

presents. Then Santa hitches it to his team of _____
                                                      ANIMAL (PLURAL)

and goes sailing through the sky. When he sees a child's house, he

lands on the _____ and slides down the chimney,
                    NOUN

landing on the _____. Then he puts the presents into the
                      NOUN

_____ that the children have hung on the
   ARTICLE OF CLOTHING (PLURAL)

mantelpiece. After he does this _____ times, he goes home to
                                      NUMBER

get ready to _____.
                  VERB

MAD LIBS® is fun to play with friends, but you can also play it by yourself! To begin with, DO NOT look at the story on the page below. Fill in the blanks on this page with the words called for. Then, using the words you have selected, fill in the blank spaces in the story.

Now you've created your own hilarious MAD LIBS® game!

# GOING TO SEE SANTA

_____ PERSON IN ROOM

_____ NUMBER

_____ PART OF THE BODY

_____ NOUN

_____ NOUN

_____ ADJECTIVE

_____ NOUN

_____ ADJECTIVE

_____ COLOR

_____ ARTICLE OF CLOTHING

_____ NOUN

_____ SILLY NOISE

_____ NOUN

_____ EXCLAMATION

_____ ANIMAL

_____ NOUN

_____ PLURAL NOUN

_____ ADVERB

# MAD LIBS®
# GOING TO SEE SANTA

Yesterday I took my friend _____ to see Santa
PERSON IN ROOM

Claus at the department store. He/She is only _____ years old,
NUMBER

so I had to be sure to hold on to his/her _____ whenever
PART OF THE BODY

we crossed a/an _____ . When we got to the _____ ,
NOUN                                   NOUN

there was a long line of _____ kids waiting to talk to Santa,
ADJECTIVE

who was sitting on a platform in the _____ department.
NOUN

Santa Claus is a big, fat _____ man with a/an _____
ADJECTIVE                               COLOR

beard who dresses in bright red _____ . Whenever a
ARTICLE OF CLOTHING

little kid came up, Santa would sit the child on his _____ and
NOUN

say, " _____ ." Then he would say, "Now have you been a good
SILLY NOISE

little _____ ?" And the kid would say, " _____ !"
NOUN                                    EXCLAMATION

Then Santa would say, "And what do you want for Christmas?" And

the kid would say, "I want a/an _____ " or "I want an electric
ANIMAL

_____ ," or "I want some little toy _____ ." Then
NOUN                                  PLURAL NOUN

Santa would say, "You bet," and the kid would run _____
ADVERB

back to his or her parents.

# THE TWELVE DAYS OF CHRISTMAS

TYPE OF BIRD _____

TYPE OF FRUIT _____

ADJECTIVE _____

NOUN _____

SOMETHING ALIVE (PLURAL) _____

NOUN _____

NUMBER _____

ADJECTIVE _____

PLURAL NOUN _____

PLURAL NOUN _____

NOUN _____

SOMETHING ROUND (PLURAL) _____

FOREIGN LANGUAGE _____

NOUN _____

# MAD LIBS®
# THE TWELVE DAYS OF CHRISTMAS

On the first day of Christmas, my true love gave to me a/an _____
TYPE OF BIRD

in a/an _____ tree. On the second day of Christmas, my true
TYPE OF FRUIT

love gave to me two _____ doves and a/an _____ in a
ADJECTIVE                                   NOUN

pear tree. On the third day of Christmas, my true love gave to me three

French _____, two turtle doves, and a/an _____
SOMETHING ALIVE (PLURAL)                                            NOUN

in a pear tree. On the fourth day of Christmas, my true love gave to

me _____ _____ _____ , three French
NUMBER        ADJECTIVE              PLURAL NOUN

_____ , two turtle doves, and a/an _____ in a pear
PLURAL NOUN                                    NOUN

tree. On the fifth day of Christmas, my true love gave to me five golden

_____ , four calling birds, three _____
SOMETHING ROUND (PLURAL)                                    FOREIGN LANGUAGE

hens, two turtle doves and a/an _____ in a pear tree.
NOUN

MAD LIBS® is fun to play with friends, but you can also play it by yourself! To begin with, DO NOT look at the story on the page below. Fill in the blanks on this page with the words called for. Then, using the words you have selected, fill in the blank spaces in the story.

Now you've created your own hilarious MAD LIBS® game!

# CHRISTMAS CAROLS

ADJECTIVE _____

ADJECTIVE _____

ADVERB _____

PLURAL NOUN _____

SILLY WORD (PLURAL) _____

PLURAL NOUN _____

NOUN _____

COLOR _____

PLACE _____

PLURAL NOUN _____

SOMETHING ALIVE (PLURAL) _____

ADJECTIVE _____

PLURAL NOUN _____

CITY _____

PLACE _____

NUMBER _____

PERSON IN ROOM _____

# MAD LIBS®
# CHRISTMAS CAROLS

This Christmas, our _____ glee club is planning a/an
                         ADJECTIVE

_____ program of Christmas carols. We all sing very
   ADJECTIVE

_____ and are going to sing on the streets and collect
   ADVERB

_____ to feed the poor, hungry _____
  PLURAL NOUN                                SILLY WORD (PLURAL)

in Transylvania. Our program will start off with "Jingle _____,"
                                                         PLURAL NOUN

followed by "Rudolph, the Red-Nosed _____," "I'm Dreaming
                                        NOUN

of a/an _____ Christmas," and "Santa Claus is Coming to
           COLOR

_____." My favorites, however, are "Deck the Halls with
     PLACE

Boughs of _____," "We Three _____ of
           PLURAL NOUN            SOMETHING ALIVE (PLURAL)

Orient Are," and "Walking in a/an _____ Wonderland." Boy,
                                   ADJECTIVE

if it goes well we can form a group, call ourselves the _____,
                                                        PLURAL NOUN

and do concerts in _____ or even in _____.
                      CITY                  PLACE

We'll have _____ fans and make a video. We'll be as famous as
             NUMBER

_____.
  PERSON IN ROOM

MAD LIBS® is fun to play with friends, but you can also play it by yourself! To begin with, DO NOT look at the story on the page below. Fill in the blanks on this page with the words called for. Then, using the words you have selected, fill in the blank spaces in the story.

Now you've created your own hilarious MAD LIBS® game!

# A TRANSYLVANIAN NEW YEAR'S

_____ ADJECTIVE

_____ NOUN

_____ NOUN

_____ SOMETHING ALIVE (PLURAL)

_____ PLURAL NOUN

_____ ADVERB

_____ PLURAL NOUN

_____ ADJECTIVE

_____ ANIMAL

_____ TYPE OF FOOD

_____ NUMBER

_____ VERB

_____ SILLY WORD

_____ NUMBER

_____ PLURAL NOUN

_____ NOUN

_____ ADJECTIVE

# MAD LIBS®
# A TRANSYLVANIAN NEW YEAR'S

New Year's Day in Transylvania is the most _____ holiday
ADJECTIVE

of the year. All the _____ shops and _____
NOUN   NOUN

factories are shut down, and the _____ dance in the
PLURAL NOUN

streets. The locals, who are called _____, spend all day
PLURAL NOUN

dancing _____. And some Transylvanians, who are called
ADVERB

_____, prepare a/an _____ feast. New Year's
PLURAL NOUN   ADJECTIVE

dinner always features a wild roast _____. It is skinned,
ANIMAL

put in an oven, and covered with _____. Then it is cooked
TYPE OF FOOD

for _____ hours. After dinner, a contest is held to see which
NUMBER

Transylvanian can _____ the loudest. The winner is
VERB

given the title of "_____." Then famous Count Dracula
SILLY WORD

himself raffles off _____ _____ to help pay the
NUMBER   PLURAL NOUN

_____ who has to come in the next day and clean up the
NOUN

whole _____ country.
ADJECTIVE

MAD LIBS® is fun to play with friends, but you can also play it by yourself! To begin with, DO NOT look at the story on the page below. Fill in the blanks on this page with the words called for. Then, using the words you have selected, fill in the blank spaces in the story.

Now you've created your own hilarious MAD LIBS® game!

# NEW YEAR'S RESOLUTIONS

NOUN _____

NOUN _____

VERB _____

TYPE OF FOOD _____

PLURAL NOUN _____

PLURAL NOUN _____

ADJECTIVE _____

PLURAL NOUN _____

VERB _____

TYPE OF LIQUID _____

PART OF THE BODY (PLURAL) _____

ARTICLE OF CLOTHING _____

ADJECTIVE _____

ADVERB _____

ADJECTIVE _____

# MAD LIBS®
# NEW YEAR'S RESOLUTIONS

I resolve that in the next year I will eat all of my _____ , just
NOUN

like my mother says. I promise to help bathe my pet _____
NOUN

and help _____ the dishes after dinner.
VERB

I will not eat any _____ that contains cholesterol or
TYPE OF FOOD

_____ . I will be polite and thoughtful and will clear the
PLURAL NOUN

_____ after meals. I will do a/an _____ deed every
PLURAL NOUN                                    ADJECTIVE

day. I will be polite to any _____ who are older than I am.
PLURAL NOUN

And I will never, never _____ my dog's tail or pour
VERB

_____ on my cat.
TYPE OF LIQUID

I will also try to brush my _____ and shine my
PART OF THE BODY

_____ every day. I promise to be really _____
ARTICLE OF CLOTHING                                    ADJECTIVE

so I can live _____ for the next 12 months. Then I'll be
ADVERB

a truly happy, _____ person.
ADJECTIVE

From CHRISTMAS FUN MAD LIBS® • Copyright © 2001, 1985 by Penguin Random House LLC.

MAD LIBS® is fun to play with friends, but you can also play it by yourself! To begin with, DO NOT look at the story on the page below. Fill in the blanks on this page with the words called for. Then, using the words you have selected, fill in the blank spaces in the story.

Now you've created your own hilarious MAD LIBS® game!

# SCROOGE

PERSON IN ROOM (FULL NAME) _____

COUNTRY _____

SOMETHING ALIVE _____

PLURAL NOUN _____

NUMBER _____

SILLY WORD _____

ADJECTIVE _____

NUMBER _____

ADJECTIVE _____

NOUN _____

NOUN _____

ADJECTIVE _____

NUMBER _____

ADJECTIVE _____

ADJECTIVE _____

NOUN _____

NAME OF PERSON _____

COLOR _____

EXCLAMATION _____

# MAD LIBS®
# SCROOGE

You have just read "A Christmas Carol" by _____ .
PERSON IN ROOM (FULL NAME)

Years ago in London, _____ , lived a mean, stingy
COUNTRY

_____ named Scrooge. He was so stingy, he saved
SOMETHING ALIVE

_____ . In fact, he had more than _____ of them. When
PLURAL NOUN                                    NUMBER

anyone mentioned Christmas, Scrooge said, "Bah! _____ ."
SILLY WORD

He had a/an _____ bookkeeper named Bob Cratchit, and
ADJECTIVE

Scrooge made him work _____ hours a day.
NUMBER

One Christmas Eve, Mr. Scrooge had a dream. He saw the Ghost of

Christmas Past, who showed him what a/an _____
ADJECTIVE

_____ he had been. Then the _____ of Christmas
NOUN                                    NOUN

Present showed Scrooge the miserable home of Bob Cratchit and

_____ Tiny Tim. Tiny Tim had a temperature of _____
ADJECTIVE                                              NUMBER

degrees. Then Scrooge met the Ghost of Christmas _____ ,
ADJECTIVE

who took him to a/an _____ cemetery, where Scrooge saw
ADJECTIVE

his own _____ . He also saw the grave of Tiny _____ .
NOUN                                              NAME OF PERSON

Scrooge turned _____ and shouted, " _____ !"
COLOR                                      EXCLAMATION

MAD LIBS® is fun to play with friends, but you can also play it by yourself! To begin with, DO NOT look at the story on the page below. Fill in the blanks on this page with the words called for. Then, using the words you have selected, fill in the blank spaces in the story.

Now you've created your own hilarious MAD LIBS® game!

# SCROOGE (CONTINUED)

SOMETHING ROUND _____

PIECE OF FURNITURE _____

NOUN _____

ADJECTIVE _____

SOMETHING ALIVE _____

ARTICLE OF CLOTHING _____

TYPE OF BIRD _____

ADJECTIVE _____

NOUN _____

TYPE OF CONTAINER _____

NOUN _____

ADJECTIVE _____

PLURAL NOUN _____

ADJECTIVE _____

PLURAL NOUN _____

ADJECTIVE _____

NOUN _____

NOUN _____

FAMOUS PERSON _____

The next morning when the _____ came up, Scrooge
SOMETHING ROUND

jumped out of his _____ and said, "I am a changed
PIECE OF FURNITURE

_____. I only hope it is not too _____ for me
NOUN   ADJECTIVE

to become a kindly, generous _____." He put on his
SOMETHING ALIVE

_____, rushed to the butcher shop, and said, "Give me
ARTICLE OF CLOTHING

the biggest _____ you have." Then he bought cakes and
TYPE OF BIRD

_____ cookies and a beautiful _____ pudding. He
ADJECTIVE   NOUN

put everything in a big _____, rushed to Bob Cratchit's
TYPE OF CONTAINER

house, and pounded on the _____. When Bob Cratchit
NOUN

opened the door, Scrooge said, "_____ Christmas, Bob.
ADJECTIVE

I have _____ for everyone, including Tiny Tim." And they
PLURAL NOUN

all had a/an _____ dinner and sang jolly _____.
ADJECTIVE   PLURAL NOUN

Scrooge had indeed changed from a/an _____ skinflint into a
ADJECTIVE

wonderful _____. He gave Tiny Tim a solid gold _____,
NOUN   NOUN

and Tiny Tim said, "Merry Christmas, and may _____
FAMOUS PERSON

bless us every one…"

MAD LIBS® is fun to play with friends, but you can also play it by yourself! To begin with, DO NOT look at the story on the page below. Fill in the blanks on this page with the words called for. Then, using the words you have selected, fill in the blank spaces in the story.

Now you've created your own hilarious MAD LIBS® game!

# THE SCHOOL PARTY

ADJECTIVE _____

NOUN _____

PERSON IN ROOM _____

NOUN _____

NOUN _____

ANOTHER PERSON IN ROOM _____

FAMOUS PERSON _____

NOUN _____

PLURAL NOUN _____

ANOTHER PERSON IN ROOM _____

NOUN _____

ADJECTIVE _____

TYPE OF FOOD _____

ANOTHER TYPE OF FOOD _____

TYPE OF LIQUID _____

ADJECTIVE _____

NUMBER _____

PLURAL NOUN _____

ANOTHER PERSON IN ROOM _____

EXCLAMATION _____

# MAD LIBS®
# THE SCHOOL PARTY

We had a/an _____ Christmas party at school last
              ADJECTIVE

year. Our _____ teacher, _____, let us use
           NOUN                  PERSON IN ROOM

the _____ room. And my favorite _____ teacher,
     NOUN                               NOUN

_____, was in charge of the decorations. We all
ANOTHER PERSON IN ROOM

drew pictures of _____ on colored paper and hung
                  FAMOUS PERSON

them on a long _____. Then we cut out stars, snowflakes,
                NOUN

and _____ and pasted them on the windows. Then
     PLURAL NOUN

_____, who is my math _____, made
ANOTHER PERSON IN ROOM              NOUN

the _____ refreshments. We had _____
     ADJECTIVE                              TYPE OF FOOD

burgers and _____ and cups of hot _____.
             ANOTHER TYPE OF FOOD              TYPE OF LIQUID

Our principal bought a really _____ tree that was
                               ADJECTIVE

_____ feet tall. And everyone put their _____ under
 NUMBER                                       PLURAL NOUN

it. _____ dressed up like Santa Claus and
    ANOTHER PERSON IN ROOM

said, " _____."
         EXCLAMATION

MAD LIBS® is fun to play with friends, but you can also play it by yourself! To begin with, DO NOT look at the story on the page below. Fill in the blanks on this page with the words called for. Then, using the words you have selected, fill in the blank spaces in the story.

Now you've created your own hilarious MAD LIBS® game!

# THANK-YOU LETTERS

NAME OF PERSON (FEMALE) _____

ADJECTIVE _____

NOUN _____

PLURAL NOUN _____

PART OF THE BODY _____

ADJECTIVE _____

ADJECTIVE _____

NAME OF PERSON (MALE) _____

NOUN _____

PLURAL NOUN _____

ADJECTIVE _____

PLURAL NOUN _____

ADJECTIVE _____

PLURAL NOUN _____

NOUN _____

CELEBRITY _____

# MAD LIBS®
# THANK-YOU LETTERS

Dear Auntie _____,
              NAME OF PERSON (FEMALE)

I want to thank you for sending me the _____ gift.
                                          ADJECTIVE

I never had a/an _____ before. I can use it to fix all my
                   NOUN

_____ . It will also keep my _____ warm
  PLURAL NOUN                                   PART OF THE BODY

if we have any _____ weather.
                  ADJECTIVE

            Your _____ nephew,
                       ADJECTIVE

            _____
                NAME OF PERSON (MALE)


Dear Grandpa and Grandma,

I really like the _____ you sent me. It must have cost
                   NOUN

a lot of _____ . All of the kids around here have
           PLURAL NOUN

_____ computers. But mine is the only one that has six
  ADJECTIVE

different _____ . It will help me do my _____
           PLURAL NOUN                            ADJECTIVE

homework, and I know I will get higher _____ this year.
                                   PLURAL NOUN

Mom says I can come to your _____ for a visit next summer.
                               NOUN

            Signed,

            _____
                 CELEBRITY

From CHRISTMAS FUN MAD LIBS® • Copyright © 2001, 1985 by Penguin Random House LLC.

**MAD LIBS®** is fun to play with friends, but you can also play it by yourself! To begin with, DO NOT look at the story on the page below. Fill in the blanks on this page with the words called for. Then, using the words you have selected, fill in the blank spaces in the story.

Now you've created your own hilarious MAD LIBS® game!

# HOLIDAY TRAVELING

SOMETHING ALIVE _____

PLURAL NOUN _____

HOLIDAY _____

PLURAL NOUN _____

TYPE OF CONTAINER _____

ADJECTIVE _____

PLACE _____

ANOTHER PLACE _____

NUMBER _____

PLURAL NOUN _____

NUMBER _____

PIECE OF FURNITURE (PLURAL) _____

PART OF THE BODY _____

ADJECTIVE _____

PLURAL NOUN _____

PLURAL NOUN _____

# MAD LIBS®
# HOLIDAY TRAVELING

During the holidays, more _____ go back home to
                            SOMETHING ALIVE (PLURAL)

visit their _____ than at any other time.  Between Christmas
            PLURAL NOUN

and _____ , the airlines pack the _____ in like
      HOLIDAY                                  PLURAL NOUN

sardines in a/an _____ . There are a lot of _____
                 TYPE OF CONTAINER                       ADJECTIVE

"no frill" airlines that will take you from _____ to
                                            PLACE

_____ for only _____ dollars.  These airlines do not
ANOTHER PLACE            NUMBER

give you any _____ . And you can only take _____
             PLURAL NOUN                              NUMBER

pieces of luggage.  They also have smaller _____ ,
                                           PIECE OF FURNITURE (PLURAL)

and you often have to sit on someone else's _____ .
                                            PART OF THE BODY

It is very _____ to travel during the holidays, but it is
           ADJECTIVE

worth it to make your _____ happy.  Don't forget to
                      PLURAL NOUN

make your _____ early.
          PLURAL NOUN

MAD LIBS® is fun to play with friends, but you can also play it by yourself! To begin with, DO NOT look at the story on the page below. Fill in the blanks on this page with the words called for. Then, using the words you have selected, fill in the blank spaces in the story.

Now you've created your own hilarious MAD LIBS® game!

# NEXT YEAR'S BOWL GAMES

ADJECTIVE _____

NOUN _____

CITY _____

ANIMAL (PLURAL) _____

ANOTHER CITY _____

ANOTHER ANIMAL (PLURAL) _____

TYPE OF FLOWER _____

CITY _____

TYPE OF BIRD (PLURAL) _____

ANOTHER CITY _____

SOMETHING ALIVE (PLURAL) _____

ANOTHER TYPE OF BIRD _____

PLURAL NOUN _____

TYPE OF VEGETABLE _____

CITY _____

ANOTHER CITY _____

ANIMAL (PLURAL) _____

NOUN _____

PERSON IN ROOM (FULL NAME) _____

TYPE OF CONTAINER _____

PART OF THE HOUSE _____

COLOR _____

# MAD LIBS®
## NEW YEAR'S
## BOWL GAMES

On New Year's Day, there are always a lot of football games. On television, they interrupt the game with commercials every few minutes. This year the _____ _____
                                                     CITY                    ANIMAL (PLURAL)
are playing the _____ _____ in the
                          A PLACE              ANIMAL (PLURAL)
famous _____ Bowl. And the _____
                 NOUN                                            CITY
_____ are matched up against the nation's
   ANIMAL (PLURAL)
number one team, the _____ _____ .
                                        CITY                  PLURAL NOUN
They will be playing in the _____ Bowl. But the game
                                          ANIMAL
that everyone is talking about is the _____ Bowl.
                                                       TYPE OF FOOD
There, the _____ Cowboys will play the hard-hitting
                    CITY
_____ _____ , whose quarterback is the
      CITY              ANIMAL (PLURAL)
super-_____ _____ . They will play in the
           NOUN              PERSON IN ROOM
fabulous Houston Astro-_____ , which has a sliding roof
                                      NOUN
and _____ AstroTurf.
         COLOR

MAD LIBS® is fun to play with friends, but you can also play it by yourself! To begin with, DO NOT look at the story on the page below. Fill in the blanks on this page with the words called for. Then, using the words you have selected, fill in the blank spaces in the story.

Now you've created your own hilarious MAD LIBS® game!

# CHRISTMAS VACATION

_____ ADJECTIVE

_____ ADJECTIVE

_____ ADJECTIVE

_____ ADJECTIVE

_____ ADJECTIVE

_____ NOUN

_____ NOUN

_____ NOUN

_____ NOUN

_____ ADJECTIVE

_____ VERB

_____ NOUN

_____ PLURAL NOUN

_____ NOUN

_____ PLURAL NOUN

_____ NOUN

_____ PLURAL NOUN

_____ NOUN

_____ PLACE

_____ COLOR

# MAD LIBS
# CHRISTMAS VACATION

This year my _____ family — my _____ sister,
ADJECTIVE                              ADJECTIVE

my _____ brother, and my parents — are planning to spend
ADJECTIVE

the holidays in the _____ mountains in a/an _____
ADJECTIVE                                          ADJECTIVE

cabin built by my _____. The cabin is in the middle of
NOUN

a huge _____ on the edge of a/an _____,
NOUN                                        NOUN

which is always frozen at this time of the _____. If the
NOUN

ice is _____ enough, we will be able to _____
ADJECTIVE                                          VERB

on it. We will decorate the big pine _____ in front of the
NOUN

cabin with Christmas _____. At night, we will build a fire
PLURAL NOUN

in the _____ and toast _____. It promises to be
NOUN                              PLURAL NOUN

a great _____. Next year I hope we can save up enough
NOUN

_____ so that we can afford to get on a/an _____
PLURAL NOUN                                            NOUN

and fly to _____ and have a really _____ Christmas.
PLACE                                        COLOR

MAD LIBS® is fun to play with friends, but you can also play it by yourself! To begin with, DO NOT look at the story on the page below. Fill in the blanks on this page with the words called for. Then, using the words you have selected, fill in the blank spaces in the story.

Now you've created your own hilarious MAD LIBS® game!

# THE NIGHT
# BEFORE CHRISTMAS

HOLIDAY _____

NOUN _____

ANIMAL_____

ANOTHER ANIMAL _____

VERB (PAST TENSE) _____

ITEM OF FURNITURE _____

TYPE OF FOOD (PLURAL) _____

VERB (PAST TENSE) _____

PART OF THE BODY (PLURAL) _____

NOUN _____

NOUN _____

PERSON IN ROOM _____

TYPE OF VEHICLE _____

NUMBER_____

ANIMAL (PLURAL)_____

ANOTHER PERSON IN ROOM_____

ANOTHER PERSON IN ROOM_____

PLURAL NOUN _____

PART OF THE BODY _____

PART OF THE BODY _____

VERB (PAST TENSE) _____

VERB (PAST TENSE) _____

ADJECTIVE _____

ADJECTIVE _____

# MAD LIBS®
# THE NIGHT
# BEFORE CHRISTMAS

'Twas the night before _____ and all through the
HOLIDAY

_____ , not a/an _____ was stirring, not even
NOUN                              ANIMAL

a/an _____ . The children were _____ all
ANOTHER ANIMAL                              VERB (PAST TENSE)

snug in their _____ , while visions of _____
ITEM OF FURNITURE                    TYPE OF FOOD (PLURAL)

_____ in their _____ . When out on the
VERB (PAST TENSE)        PART OF THE BODY (PLURAL)

lawn there arose such a clatter, I sprang from my _____ to
NOUN

see what was the matter. I knew in a/an _____ it must be
NOUN

Saint _____ , with his miniature _____ and
PERSON IN ROOM                          TYPE OF VEHICLE

_____ tiny _____ named Dasher and Dancer and
NUMBER              ANIMAL (PLURAL)

_____ and _____ . He filled all our
ANOTHER PERSON IN ROOM        ANOTHER PERSON IN ROOM

_____ , then laying his _____ aside of his
PLURAL NOUN                    PART OF THE BODY

_____ , up the chimney he _____ . But I heard
PART OF THE BODY              VERB (PAST TENSE)

him exclaim, as he _____ out of sight, " _____
VERB (PAST TENSE)                        ADJECTIVE

Christmas to all and to all a/an _____ night."
ADJECTIVE

Download on the
App Store

GET IT ON
Google Play

## Download Mad Libs today!

Join the millions of Mad Libs fans
creating wacky and wonderful
stories on our apps!